D0546608

RAINBOW
GARDEN

RAINBOW GARDEN

by

Patricia M. St. John

Member of the North Africa Mission, working with the Tulloch Memorial Hospital in Tangier, Morocco.

moody press
chicago

© Copyright 1960 by Patricia St. John
American edition by permission

American Publisher's Note:
  At the request of the publishers in Great Britain, we have
reprinted this book without any revisions.

ISBN 0-8024-0028-0

37 39 40 38 36

Printed in the United States of America

THIS BOOK
IS DEDICATED TO
HAZEL AND MICHAEL

CONTENTS

CHAPTER I

LAND OF SUNSHINE

IT ALL BEGAN one cold January night, when I was kneeling in front of my mother's electric fire, drying my hair. Outside, the snow was falling over London, and the footsteps and the noise of the traffic were muffled, but inside my mother's pink bedroom, with the velvet curtains drawn close and the shaded lamps casting down rosy light, we were very warm and snug.

I was enjoying myself, for it was one of those very rare evenings when my mother was at home and seemed to have nothing to do, except attend to me. This was so unusual that at first we had not quite known what to say to each other, but we had watched television, and then she had brought out a pile of magazines full of dress patterns and had let me choose a new summer frock. After that she had washed my hair and sat on a little stool curling it, while I watched in the long mirror and ate chocolates.

It should have been a delightful evening. Mrs.

Moody, the housekeeper, had a day off and had gone home to Golders Green, and the flat somehow seemed brighter without her. I was fond of Mrs. Moody, who looked after me far more than my mother did, but she was not a very cheerful person to have about, because, being elderly and old-fashioned, she strongly disapproved of me. She disapproved of Mummy because she went to so many parties and stayed out so late at night and got up so late in the morning. Mrs. Moody, in her young days, went to bed at ten and got up at six, and no nonsense, but as Mummy usually went to bed at two and got up at ten, I couldn't see that she was really any lazier than Mrs. Moody. Both spent exactly the same numbers of hours in bed.

Mrs. Moody disapproved of me too, because she thought I had too many party frocks and too many cream cakes for tea. I had heard her tell the cook in the flat downstairs that I should grow up a butterfly like my mother, but although she said it in a disapproving voice, I was pleased, for butterflies were beautiful and gay; I had watched them flitting about in the sunshine on the tulips in St. James's Park. Cook had replied that, for all my finery, I was a plain little piece; but I didn't understand what she meant and thought she must be talking about the cake she was making.

"Mummy," I said, tossing back my hair and looking up at her, "you still haven't told me what day I'm going back to school. It must be soon now."

My mother was silent for some minutes, and I began to wonder what was the matter. I had asked twice before, and she had changed the subject.

"When, Mummy?" I repeated impatiently. "It must be some day next week, and Mrs. Moody hasn't looked at my uniform yet, and I know my gym. tunic needs letting down."

My mother seemed intent on my curls. Then, instead of answering this simple question, she suddenly said, "Elaine, would you like to go to the country?"

I twisted my head round and stared at her. "The country?" I repeated. "Why, where? Do you mean instead of going to school?"

"Well, no," replied my mother, "not exactly. I mean, you'd go to school in the country, and I'm sure you'd love it when Spring comes. The thing is, Elaine, I've got the offer of a marvellous job, but it means travelling about and going abroad, and I just can't take you with me. Besides, it is a secretarial job, and I shall be frightfully busy."

"Well," I said after thinking it over for a few

minutes, "I think I'd really rather stay here with Mrs. Moody. I'd be at school all day, and we'd be all right in the evenings. You'd be home for the holidays, wouldn't you?"

"But, darling," answered my mother rather impatiently, because she always liked everyone to agree with her plans at once, "you don't *understand!* We couldn't possibly afford to keep on the flat and Mrs. Moody just for you. You'll simply love it in the country, and there is such a nice family who are willing to have you. They've got six children, and there is a girl called Janet who is only a few months younger than you."

"But if you give up the flat and Mrs. Moody," I said blankly, "where will my home be? I mean, I shan't belong anywhere."

My mother gave a little shrug of annoyance, and I knew she thought I was being naughty and difficult, but I couldn't help it. I didn't particularly mind Mummy going, for I never saw her much, in any case. But Mrs. Moody and the flat was a different matter. I should be like a stray cat and not belong anywhere. Besides, if I did go to the country and didn't like it, or if those six children proved objectionable, where should I come back to?

"Don't be silly, Elaine," pleaded my mother.

"Of course when I come back we'll get a new home, and you'll always belong to me. Do try and be sensible. I don't want to leave you, but it will be much better for you later on, if I earn more instead of just this part-time job I've been doing. Besides, I've always wanted to go abroad, and this is a marvellous chance."

I sat staring into the red glow of the stove, my mouth closed in an obstinate line. Six children in the country sounded very fierce and dangerous to me; I didn't want to go at all.

My mother was quite put out by my silence. She started again in a coaxing voice:

"You've no idea how nice it will be," she urged. "And I've taken such trouble over finding a really nice place for you. Mrs. Owen was at school with me, and although we didn't keep up, I liked her better than any other girl I knew. Then when your Daddy was killed, she wrote to me. She saw the news of the plane crash in the paper, and she wanted to know all about you and asked if she could be of any help. Of course, you were only tiny then, but I wrote to her a little while ago and asked if she knew of a nice boarding school, and she answered by return of post offering to have you in her home, so that you could go to day school with Janet. It was very, very good of her, Elaine, and you must try and be a sensible girl. France isn't far away, and I shall come over and see you from time to time."

I could not explain that that was not the part I minded, because I was quite used to not seeing my mother. So I just sat silent, but I could see her face by glancing in the mirror, and it was clear that she was worried and frowning.

"Elaine," she said suddenly, "I'm going to have a little party to-morrow night to say goodbye to a few friends. You shall help get ready, and then you can dress up in your best party dress and come to the beginning of it. Won't that be fun?"

I looked up quickly. "To-morrow? Already?" I cried. "Then when are we going?"

"Well," said my mother hesitatingly, "there'll be such a lot to do packing up the flat, I thought you'd better go fairly soon. I told Mrs. Owen you'd go on Friday."

"Friday!" I thought to myself, "and to-day is Tuesday—just three more days!" I suddenly felt terribly lonely and forlorn, but I wasn't allowed to say No, and it didn't seem much good making a fuss when it was all settled. Nor did there seem anything else to talk about, so I escaped as soon as I could and crept away to bed. When Mummy came to say goodnight, I pretended to be asleep.

Next day was busy and gay, and I almost forgot my fears in the preparations for the party. The guests were coming at 8:30, and by half-past seven I was all ready in my pink frilly dress with my hair carefully curled. I had never been to a grown-up party before, and I wondered what we'd do.

I was disappointed on the whole, for although everyone made a fuss of me to begin with, they very soon forgot about me. There were no other children, and we didn't play games, although I think they were going to play cards later on. They sat about having refreshments and smoking and making jokes I couldn't understand, but they must have been very funny, because everyone laughed so much. Mummy talked about Mrs. Moody and called her an absolute treasure, but oh, so dreary!—and they all screamed with laughter, which surprised me, for I did not know that Mrs. Moody was funny. I suddenly found that I felt rather dizzy from the heat and smoke, and a little sick from the cream cake I'd eaten. Mummy was busy pouring out drinks, and I didn't think anyone would notice if I went away.

At the next burst of laughter I slipped out and went into the kitchen. Mrs. Moody at least had not forgotten me. She was sitting in an armchair mending my socks. "Come along, Elaine," she said sharply, "it's more than high time you were in bed. You're half asleep!"

I still felt queer, and leaned up against her. "Come with me, Mrs. Moody," I whispered rather shamefacedly, "I feel sick!'"

"And small wonder, such goings-on at your age," retorted Mrs. Moody, rising at once. But she put her arm round me very gently and led me to my room, and helped me out of my party finery into my nightgown. Then she fetched me a hot-water bottle because I was shivering, and brushed my hair while I lay with my head on the pillow.

"Mrs. Moody," I said suddenly, "I'm going to the country, and Mummy's going to France."

Mrs. Moody bristled and pursed her lips, but whether France or the country was the subject of her disapproval I had yet to find out.

"So I am given to understand," she replied stiffly, but she was smoothing my curls very tenderly.

"Mrs. Moody, I whispered coaxingly, "have you ever lived in the country?"

A slow smile spread over Mrs. Moody's face. Apparently it was safe to talk about the country —it was France that musn't be mentioned.

"I was brought up in Sussex," said Mrs. Moody, "in a little cottage with a garden full of lavender and sweet peas and roses. To my mind, it's a better place than London for children."

I snuggled closer. It sounded like the nicest kind of story. In my imagination I could see the little girl that was Mrs. Moody, thin and straight-backed and solemn, with her hair screwed back behind her ears, framed in rose bushes.

"Go on," I whispered, "tell me more."

She gave one of her rare little chuckles.

"I can't remember much about it now, Elaine," she said, "except the swallows making nests under the thatch, and the stream where we used to play, all golden like with kingcups—and the posies we used to pick. My granddad knew all the names of the wild flowers, and we children used to laugh at them—funny they were . . . cuckoo's stockings, milkmaids, creeping jenny, granny's nightcaps. Pretty, I thought them!"

A burst of laughter exploded across the passage. I nestled closer to Mrs. Moody. We seemed shut in by ourselves in a land of sweet memories.

"Mrs. Moody," I said pleadingly, "why don't you come with me?"

"Because I'm not invited, love," she answered, "and you're a big girl now. I've got another place as housekeeper, but I shall miss you, dearie, to be sure I shall."

"Go on about the country, then," I said, and she chatted on about lambs and cows and fruit picking and orchards. I felt cool and well again, and I lay listening until I fell asleep with her work-worn hands clasped tightly in mine. It seemed as though, now that I was going to the country, Mrs. Moody disapproved of me no longer.

CHAPTER II

THE WELCOME

THE NEXT DAY FLEW BY, and my mother was kinder to me and took more notice of me than ever before. She spent a lot of time with me and took me out shopping, and in the afternoon we had tea at Selfridge's and went on to a pantomime. It was most exciting, and in the daytime I almost forgot the presence of Mrs. Moody, who sat solidly in the kitchen sorting and marking and letting down my clothes. Only at night, when Mummy left me with a hurried kiss and went off to her evening engagement, did Mrs. Moody become important.

It was not difficult those last nights to persuade her to come and sit by my bed in the dark and to go on talking about the country, and this was a good thing, for it was only after dark that I began to feel that the world was really a very unsafe place and that in a very short time I should really belong to nobody; I should be shut up with six children whether I liked them or not, and whether they liked me or not, and down at the bottom of my heart I knew that the children at school did not like me much, and I sometimes wondered why. No one had ever told me that I was spoiled and vain and cared for no one but myself—except Mrs. Moody when she was cross, and I had not taken any notice of her.

But there was this much to allay my fears. I had always been to the seaside in August, though it was a towny sort of seaside, and I knew nothing whatever about the country. Yet from Mrs. Moody's gentle talk I gathered that it was a magic place where roses and lavender bloomed all the year round, and the sun shone every day. I suppose her memories of Sussex were only of summer days, and we both forgot that I was going up to North Wales in the middle of a particularly cold January. As it was, I half imagined that I was going to be transported to a bright world of flowers; and this was pleasant, for the snow had melted in the London streets, and the pavements were thick with brown slush and the air was heavy with fog.

Mrs. Moody remembered more and more as the week passed. She told me about harvests and hayfields, sheep dipping and fox hunting, and I would lie listening, clinging to her hand and feeling immensely comforted. When at last the dreaded morning came and the taxi stood at the door to take me to Euston, I realised with dismay that it was far worse saying goodbye to Mrs. Moody than to Mummy; and when we turned the corner and lost sight of her thin figure in its ugly apron waving on the doorstep, I felt that I had been suddenly cut off from all that made life safe and I burst into tears.

My mother, who was in the taxi with me, was upset and put out by my sobs, and implored me to be good and sensible, so, as usual, I dried my tears and kept my fears to myself. At Euston we went to the bookstall and bought some of my favourite comics, and two big boxes of chocolates, one for myself to eat in the train and one for the little Owens. This pleased me very much, and when the whistle blew and the train steamed off, I was able to wave quite cheerfully. In fact, I was impatient to be off, so that I could settle down and enjoy the journey.

Mummy had put me in the charge of a lady who was travelling to Ireland, but I was not a friendly sort of child and, as I took no notice of her, she soon gave up trying to take notice of me. I read my comics and munched my sandwiches and chocolates, and now and then I went and stood in the corridor and looked out of the window; what I saw filled me with dismay, for this country was nothing like Mrs. Moody's country. It was miles of wet, yellow fields and bare black hedges and trees, with the distances blotted out by mist. It looked cold and muddy and lonely and wretched, and I soon tired of it. I curled up in my corner and went fast asleep.

If it hadn't been for the lady looking after me, I should have slept right through the stop where I was supposed to get out. As it was, she woke me just in time, and I tumbled out with my big case and stood waiting on the platform, still half asleep and very bewildered and cold. The train roared away almost immediately, and the first thing I noticed was the quietness—no traffic or footsteps, only the muffled sound of the sea on the other side of the station, and the soft rattle of waves breaking on pebbles, and when I sniffed I found that the air smelt salt and clean.

But no sooner had I realised that the sea was only a few yards away than I looked up and saw a woman hurrying towards me as fast as three little children clinging to her hands and coat would allow, and one was only a toddler. They had been waiting for me at the far end of the platform, which was some distance away, and I supposed they were the Owens. I did not go forward to meet them, but stood quite still by my case.

"How do you do, Mrs. Owen?" I remarked stiffly, trying to imitate my mother's company voice when she greeted visitors whom she didn't like, and I held out my small, gloved hand.

Mrs. Owen hesitated, surprised, and there was just a second's silence as we stared at each other in the dim light of that January afternoon. Then a look came into her face that I did not understand—she might have been going to laugh, or she might have been going to cry; in any case, she brushed aside my hand and kissed me very gently on both cheeks.

"How nice you've come, Elaine," she said, "we've all been so excited, and Peter and Janet were so cross they couldn't get home in time from school to meet you; but Johnny and Frances and Robin have come, and the others are waiting at home—now come along, the taxi's just outside."

Johnny and Frances and Robin seemed as doubtful of me as I was of them, and had backed to the other side of their mother. I suppose they expected me to speak to them or kiss them, but I knew nothing about little children, and they were far smaller than I—in fact, in their woolly hoods and overcoats and strong country shoes they all looked as broad as they were tall. When we reached the taxi they all tumbled into the back seat and started whispering to each other under a rug. I sat in the front with Mrs. Owen and answered Yes and No to her questions, and felt quite overcome with shyness and desolation.

The landscape, once we left the little town, was the gloomiest I'd ever seen in my life. It was a cold, drizzly twilight, and the trees and hills were still blotted out. I could see nothing but wet roads, yellow fields, black hedges, and not a soul in sight. Whatever did one do here all day?

I stopped listening to Mrs. Owen and stared out of the window. The little ones kept peeping out from under the rug like rabbits and giggling and disappearing again. I think it was their way of trying to make friends, but I took no notice of them.

"There's our house," cried Johnny suddenly, poking me rather painfully in the back and pointing ahead, and I followed his finger, suddenly interested. We had been driving between trees, but now we were out in the open country again, and there on the hillside beamed the uncurtained orange windows of a house; they were the only lights to be seen in that direction, for the house stood apart from the village, and they looked warm and friendly and welcoming. I glanced timidly at Mrs. Owen, and she smiled.

"Welcome to the Vicarage, Elaine," she said. "Here we are at home."

As the taxi drew up at the gate, the front door was flung open, and two sturdy children and a big collie tumbled down the path with a tremendous lot of noise. I hated hearty, rough children and shrank back into my corner. But they didn't seem to notice, for they were prancing excitedly round their mother, and when at last I did climb out, the dog leaped up and put his front paws on my shoulders and tried to lick my face. The children shouted with delight, for this was apparently what they had taught him to do, but I thought he was going to bite me, and screamed with terror. Mrs. Owen rescued me in a moment and calmed the commotion.

"He's just greeting you, Elaine," explained Janet, "and he can shake hands too. Hold out your hand, and he'll hold out his paw. He's a very polite dog."

But I thought he was a horrible dog and backed away, which surprised the children, for they could not imagine anyone being afraid of Cadwaller.

I saw Janet and Peter glance at each other in amused surprise as we somehow all made our way up the garden path and in at the front door. It was clear I had made a bad beginning.

"You are sleeping with me," said Janet kindly, making another attempt at a welcome. "I'll show you where and help you unpack," and she led the way upstairs, and Peter came behind carrying my case. She flung open the door of a little bedroom with two beds side by side.

I was not pleased, nor did I pretend to be. In London I had had a bedroom to myself with an electric fire, and a thick carpet on the floor, and my own little oak bookcase and armchair and toy cupboard. This seemed to me a cold shabby little room, and I did not notice all the tokens of welcome strewn about it that the children had prepared so carefully—the budding hyacinth on the chest of drawers, Frances's dearest teddy reclining on my bed, Peter's favourite picture of a battleship stuck on the wall above my pillow, and the little moss garden arranged in a tin lid on my chair.

Janet watched me eagerly, but I gave no sign of pleasure, and then the expectant look died from her face, and she shyly pointed out my bed and drawers, and said she'd better go and help

Mummy get supper. I felt she was glad to leave me, and I was glad to be left. I looked distastefully round at the rather shabby bedside mats and faded curtains and bedspreads, and then I noticed two sticky boiled sweets and a faded sprig of winter jessamine reposing on my pillow. I flung them angrily into the waste-paper basket. Mummy and Mrs. Moody would never have allowed rubbish to be left on visitors' pillows, and I didn't see why Mrs. Owen should either. I opened my case and began hanging up my dresses in the cupboard that I was to share with Janet, and I was pleased to see that my clothes were much prettier than hers. I laid out my new smocked nightie in full view on the bed; perhaps I could show her a thing or two, even if I was frightened of dogs.

But just as I was arranging the frills, Mrs. Owen came in and sat down with the youngest member of the family on her lap—a round bouncing baby of ten months with big blue eyes.

"This is baby Lucy," said Mrs. Owen, "and I hope you like babies, because I'm counting on your help. Six children is a lot, and you'll be my eldest girl. You are eleven, aren't you?"

"Yes," I answered, staring at baby Lucy, who suddenly gurgled and broke into a smile that showed two teeth. It had not occurred to me that

I should be expected to help. At home Mrs. Moody did all the work, and I amused myself and watched television and read books. I was not sure if I liked the idea or not; helping with a baby might be fun. In any case I could try, and if I didn't like it, I wouldn't do it, for I intended to be happy in my own way. And to me happiness meant having what I wanted and doing what I liked. Of any other sort of happiness I knew nothing.

I followed Mrs. Owen down to supper, after watching her tuck up baby Lucy in her cot, and was relieved to see that the large potato pie was carried in by a rosy-cheeked girl called Blodwen. I was afraid they had no maid, and then I might be expected to wash up or dust, which I should not have liked at all and had no intention of doing.

When the meal was ready, Mr. Owen appeared from his study. He was a tall, round-shouldered man with a tired face and kind blue eyes. He picked up Robin, who had flung his arms round his father's knees and nearly sent him flying, and greeted me very warmly. Then he said grace, and we sat down amidst a babel of voices, for Mr. Owen had only just come in from visiting his parishioners, and as Peter and Janet had not seen him since breakfast, there was a tremendous lot of news to be imparted. Johnny and Frances seemed to have done a great deal since dinner-time, too, and were bursting with information.

"Daddy," began Peter, who had only gone back to school that day, "I'm sitting next to Glyn Evans in class, and he said he'd swop me two rabbits, for some stamps and a catapult—may I, Daddy?"

"Daddy," broke in Janet, not waiting for a reply, "I might be in the under-twelve netball team; do you think we could put up a post in the garden, so I could practice shooting?"

"May I, Daddy?" said Peter.

"Daddy, Daddy," squeaked Johnny, suddenly remembering and going rigid with excitement, "we stood on the bridge when the train went underneath, and all the smoke came up round us."

"Could I, Daddy?" persisted Janet.

"There were two baby lambs in the field, I heard them cry," said Frances in a whisper that reached her father's ears above all the noise. She smiled rapturously at him, confident that her bit of news was perhaps the most exciting of all, and he smiled back at her, understanding all the sweetness of the first whispers of spring to a five-year-old.

"May I, Daddy?" said Peter again. He was a very persevering boy, as I discovered later.

"Could I, Daddy?" said Janet at the same moment.

"Why, yes, I should think so," answered Mr. Owen peacefully. "There's an old post in the garage, Jan, we could fix up with some wire, and I'll see if I can find a box and some netting for your rabbits, Pete. What about you, Elaine? Do you play netball?"

"I used to sometimes at school," I mumbled, wishing they would leave me alone. I felt terribly shy of all these happy, confident children, and I wished Janet wasn't so keen about netball. I'd never liked games much. I'd sat at home in the holidays or gone to shops with my mother, and I'd never learned to run about and jump and play.

I didn't like the potato pie either; it was too stodgy, and I wanted to go home. My eyes filled with tears that might have fallen, had I not suddenly realised that Frances was looking at me in a secret kind of way, her homely little face alight with suppressed excitement.

"Did you see them?" she suddenly whispered across the table, under cover of a loud discussion that had just arisen between Peter and Janet as to whether they wanted white rabbits or brown rabbits, he-rabbits or she-rabbits, old rabbits or young rabbits—there seemed to be an endless choice.

"What?" I whispered back shyly.

"Them, my s'prise," she answered softly, her eyes shining. "What I put on your pillow—did you see?"

I suddenly remembered the sticky sweets and the withered twig. I had thought them rubbish, but now they suddenly seemed precious. The token that one, at least, of this rowdy gang had cared about my coming.

"Yes," I answered, "I did ... thank you, Frances."

Then I was suddenly aware of a hush, and I noticed that Johnny had laid a Bible in front of the minister. He was about to read, and a strange calm seemed to settle over those restless, eager children. I had always thought the Bible a very dull book, but to-night everyone appeared to be listening, even little Frances.

I did not attempt to listen, for I was certain I couldn't understand if I tried. It was something about a vine and some branches, but only the last verse caught my attention.

"These things have I spoken unto you, that your joy might be full."

I turned these words over in my mind, for I liked the sound of them, and then everyone shut their eyes and bowed their heads to pray, and this I understood, for Mrs. Moody used sometimes to make me say, "Our Father, Which art in Heaven." But in a moment I realised that this was different, for Mr. Owen seemed to be speaking to Someone Who was there, and his prayer seemed to gather us all into a place of safety—Mummy far away in London, the children round the table, the babies asleep upstairs, all brought near to Someone Who cared and Who could make us good and happy.

An hour later, when Mrs. Owen had kissed us goodnight and Janet had fallen asleep beside me, I lay wakeful, staring out of the window at the starry sky that looked so wide without any roofs and spires massed against it. I felt quite bewildered by all that had happened, and it seemed years since the taxi had turned the corner, hiding Mrs. Moody from view. Once again my eyes filled with tears of desolation, and I wanted to go home—and yet there were those strange words that seemed to breathe a promise of comfort: "These things have I spoken unto you, that your joy might be full."

What things? I wondered.

I wished I'd listened.

CHAPTER III

THE OTHER SIDE OF THE MIST

WHEN I WOKE NEXT MORNING, Janet, fully dressed, was roaming round the room making preparations for a Saturday at home, and the moment she saw my eyes open she started talking. Her shyness seemed to have vanished overnight, and while I dressed, she sat on her bed jigging up and down and telling me all about their games and secrets. By breakfast-time I had ceased to wonder what one did all day in the country. In fact, I could not think how these children managed to crowd so much adventure into twelve short hours.

Breakfast being over, everyone helped and seemed to enjoy it. Janet and Frances fought for the job of feeding Lucy, who had been amusing us all breakfast by trying to push her fat cheeks through the bars of her pen and making fierce noises. They got quite excited, and I feared that Lucy might get pulled in half. But Mrs. Owen put her head round the door and reminded them that it was Frances's turn, whereupon Frances, who loved Janet dearly, went all generous and said Janet could do it, and Janet said, No, Frances could, and she'd help Blodwen—and off she went, leaving me wondering what all the noise had been about.

The boys had gone off to bring in firewood, Mrs. Owen had gone into the kitchen, and it was suddenly very quiet. There was no sound at all except the sucky, gurgly sound of Lucy eating her cornflour, and Frances's soft little voice telling her stories as I stood looking out of the window. It was a drizzly day, and I could still see nothing beyond the garden gate but rising yellow fields and black trees. The distances were still veiled in mist, and yet it was a thin, bright mist with the promise of sunshine behind it, and I found myself wondering almost eagerly what I should see when the curtains parted. Would I see more endless stretches of fields and hedges, or was there a brighter land and a blue sky beyond the mist? And as I stood wondering, a bird started singing very loud and sweet, somewhere from the mystery of that hidden country.

I was startled out of my dreams by the touch of Mrs. Owen's hand on my shoulder.

"Elaine, dear," she said, "when you've made your own bed, will you come and help me with the little ones' beds? And then the children want to get out and play, and I expect you'd like to go with them."

I looked up surprised and not very pleased. For one thing, I did not see why I, as a visitor, should be expected to make my own bed; Mrs. Moody always made it at home. Also, whatever would we do out of doors on a cold, damp day like this? But I had learned, in my short life, to keep silent about what I thought, so I followed Mrs. Owen upstairs and applied myself to the task of bedmaking, but I had been used to a centrally heated flat and electric fires, and I found the bedrooms horribly cold. I shivered and looked sulky.

"It is cold in the country compared with London," said Mrs. Owen, "but you'll soon get used to it. You need to run about and keep moving, and you'll get as rosy as Janet. This is the bleakest time of the year, you know, Elaine, but Spring is on the way. Every day is getting longer and lighter, and we shall soon have the flowers coming out. You'll love it then."

And then suddenly she started talking about my mother at school, and that was really interesting. I listened eagerly and laughed, and felt quite disappointed when a sort of surging and clattering in the hall below announced that the children were ready to go out.

Johnny came dashing upstairs, his boots crashing into the carpet rods.

"Mummy," he shouted, "I found a dead bunny, and we're going to have a funeral. Have you got a boot-box?"

"Really?" said Mrs. Owen a little anxiously, "not a very dead bunny, is it, Janet?"

"No, Mummy," answered Janet reassuringly, "a just dead one—it was still warm."

"Well, don't touch it," said their mother, hurrying down with newspapers and a broken cardboard box. "Wrap it up in this paper and some big leaves, and put it in here. There now, don't touch it again, and Johnny, wash your hands."

"I'm not playing funerals," announced Peter grandly. "It's a game for babies. I'm going tree-climbing."

"Oh, no, Peter," cried Janet anxiously, "we always play something with the little ones first. You needn't be in the procession. You can go and dig the grave and ring the bell, and I'll be the clergyman. We must do what the babies like sometimes. We'll climb trees after."

Janet, as I discovered later, adored funerals and wouldn't have missed it for anything, and the moment Peter had gone off to do as he was told she started organising in good earnest.

"Get leaves and jessamine, everyone," she ordered, "and make the box pretty."

She was interrupted by Robin, who burst into our midst very red in the face after a struggle with Blodwen and his wellingtons. He did not know what a funeral was, but he was terrified of missing it.

"Wobin's comin' to the fun'al," he chanted joyously, "and Jumbo—Janny, Jumbo's comin' to the fun'al too."

"All right," said Janet kindly, "you can drive the boot-box, Robs! Jumbo's a black horse with plumes, and we'll tie the box to his tail with string. You can lead Jumbo at the head of the procession, and I'll be the taxi-driver and come behind with Francie and Johnnie in the wheelbarrow."

"But you are the clergyman," objected Frances.

"Not till I get there," explained Janet. "Oh, there's Elaine too! I forgot her. You can walk behind and carry flowers, Elaine."

"There aren't any," I said coldly. I thought they were all quite mad.

"Get a yew bough, then," said Janet, pointing to the tree by the gate, "and let's start. Peter's getting angry."

We went very slowly, because Jumbo, a strange, shapeless, stuffed woolen affair with four legs, a trunk, and a tail sticking out in all directions, was being walked step by step down the path with the box thumping behind him. Peter was banging the dinner bell impatiently from behind the laurel hedge, and in the end the taxi-driver got impatient too and raced the taxi round the hearse and tipped both the mourners into the sprouts. This upset the hearse-driver very much indeed, and he had to be comforted with a peanut out of the grave-digger's pocket before the funeral could proceed.

I was surprised at what I saw round the corner of the laurel hedge. There was a neat little animal cemetery with tiny graves surrounded by pebbles and marked with wooden crosses. On some the name had been carved with a penknife and filled in with Indian ink. There were graves for thrushes and rabbits, a squirrel, a mouse, and Blackout the kitten, and at the far end a freshly dug hole lined with laurel leaves all ready for poor Bunny, who was laid carefully inside. Frances sprinkled a few winter daisies, and when it had been covered, Janet preached a sermon about rabbits to the two mourners and myself. The grave-digger had walked away, and the hearse-driver was making a mud pie for Jumbo.

"Now we'll sing a hymn," said Frances, as the sermon drew to a close. "We'll sing that hymn we learned in Sunday School,

"Around the throne of God in Heaven
Thousands of children stand."

"Shall we sing 'Thousands of rabbits stand' instead?" asked Johnny.

"Certainly not," said the clergyman hastily, "it would be very naughty," but she started giggling helplessly, and in the end the mourners sang their hymn alone, and very small and plaintive it sounded, rising in the still mist.

"Come along now," said Janet, as the last notes died away. "We'll find Pete and go to the tree. We've got some plans to make."

She picked up the wheelbarrow and gave Robin and Jumbo a ride, and I followed. Only Frances lingered, making daisy chains for the new grave. She loved the little cemetery, for to Frances the grave was nothing but a long passage down which the buried one walked for a long time until he reached the gate of Heaven. And there, whether you knocked with your paw, or tapped with your beak, or scratched with your claws, the door was flung open, and you were welcomed in to fields of sunshine and everlasting flowers, where nothing hurt or killed or destroyed. But of course I knew nothing about this at the time; I just wondered why Frances lingered on alone, kneeling on the damp earth under the laurel hedge, intent on her daisy chain.

Mugs of cocoa and ginger biscuits were served out of the kitchen window at that point, and then we all set out again, leaving Robin under the kitchen table with the cat and collecting Cadwaller in his place. Cadwaller was not allowed at funerals, for once, when he was meant to be a mourner, he had had the bad taste to try and eat the rabbit who was about to be buried.

Peter had gone on ahead and we hurried after him, joined at the gate by Frances. We ran along a muddy path bounded by great silver-trunked beeches, and found him already seated on a low bough dangling his legs and carving the bark with his penknife. He called to us to hurry, announcing that he would be working on his rabbit hutch all the afternoon, and there was no time to spare.

"Frances first," ordered Peter, lying flat on his tummy along the branch. Janet gave her a lift, and Peter seized her hands and hauled. Once astride the branch, tiny Frances proceeded to climb hand over hand up into the heights, like a nimble squirrel. Johnny did the same.

I was seized with horror, for I'd never climbed a tree in my life and was certain I never could.

"Come on, Elaine," said Peter kindly," you can easily reach alone. Jump, and kick up your legs and wiggle round."

But I knew I could do nothing of the kind. I should make a fool of myself and get hurt. I turned my back on him.

"No, thank you," I called over my shoulder, "I don't like climbing trees; it's babyish. I'm going home to unpack."

I did not turn round to see how this remark was taken, but there was complete silence for a moment or two. Then Peter said, "Oh, never mind her, Jan, she's too stuck up for us. Jump, and I'll give you a pull."

I walked home slowly, half blind with the tears I was too proud to let fall. These children, I thought, would never like me. I should never like them, or their silly baby games, and I felt terribly sorry for myself. That I should pay the price of learning to do what I didn't like or practising what I was afraid of doing, never occurred to me.

"I hate the country, and I hate Peter," I muttered to myself. "I shall write to Mummy and tell her I'm very, very unhappy, and I want to go home at once. I shan't stay in a place where I'm unhappy. Why should I?"

I had reached the top of the little slope, and I glanced backwards. The four were sitting on a high bough dangling their legs like a row of happy monkeys. They were all very close together and probably all talking at once. How stupid they were! Yet the sight of their stupidity made me feel still more wretched, for it was so lonely being sensible.

But as I looked, I noticed something else. The sun had begun to scatter the mist and was shining through triumphantly. Through the bright, thinning veil I could see a broad, rolling land, and now wherever I looked, the sun was winning, and the mist was flying like puffs of smoke against the blue and wreathing like ragged scarves in the branches of the trees. I gazed round me, and everywhere the curtain was becoming transparent, and I could see high hills rising behind ploughed acres and dappled copses, while in front of me lay the long stretch of the sea between two headlands.

The birds were singing too. On a holly tree near by a robin puffed out his breast and trilled for joy—and his breast was as scarlet as the berries. Everywhere I turned I could hear chirps and twitterings and the laughter of birds waiting for spring. For a moment I almost felt happy.

But how could I be happy when no one bothered about me, and I couldn't do what I liked? The fields round me, wet with mist, seemed suddenly to have turned silver and the blue air sparkled, but my eyes were too blinded with tears to see the light; only from the holly tree the robin kept singing.

CHAPTER IV

THE FOOT OF THE RAINBOW

I SHALL NEVER FORGET my first Sunday in the country.

Sundays at home had been a little dismal: Mrs. Moody always arrayed herself in a majestic black hat and went off to spend an hour in an ugly brick building down the road; she always returned in a particularly disapproving mood, shaking her head and sniffing; Mummy nearly always stayed in bed for the morning and went out after tea. I had often found it a long, lonely day.

But here everyone dressed up in their brightest and best, and I learned to my surprise that we were all going to Church. We set out at a quarter to eleven along a muddy footpath that led through the fields, and though it was misty again, the birds were still singing in the mist. Peter had gone ahead with his father, and I was glad of that, for, never having had anything to do with little boys, I disliked him very much indeed. Janet danced nearly all the way, skipping over puddles and tufts of grass, and Johnny and Frances clung to their mother's hands, both talking hard all the time and neither seeming to expect any answer. Blodwen had stayed at home, for it was her turn to look after Robin and Lucy.

I walked a little apart, wishing I hadn't got to go to Church. I was sure it would be very dull indeed, and I could not see why children should be bothered with it. But the bell clanged insistently through the mist, and we had soon reached the wooden gate where people were waiting to greet Mrs. Owen, whom they all knew and loved. We were early, and they lingered for a few minutes chatting, and as I stood quietly by, waiting, I noticed something that made me give a little gasp.

For the old churchyard was a mass of snowdrops, thick on the graves and clumped in the rough grass. I moved off to see them more closely and, forgetting everyone, I stooped down to examine them. There were transparent buds still sheathed and wide open flowers; never before had I seen such spotless beauty and purity.

They were clumped in peculiar thickness round a very old grave-stone leaning backwards, and the inscription was so beaten and worn by the weather that I could hardly read it. Most of the stones were inscribed in Welsh, but this one was in English, and I tried to spell out the words between the sprays of ivy that trailed across it: "David Davies", I spelt slowly, "1810-1880. In . . ." But the next words were completely worn away. Only with difficulty could I make out the end: "is fulness of joy".

I gave a little start, for I had heard those words before—at least, not quite, but nearly; they were like the verse Mr. Owen had read, but this sounded even better. "In . . . somewhere . . . is fulness of joy."

What could the missing words be? Where could fulness of joy be found?

But as I stood there dreaming, Janet suddenly gave me a friendly thump on the back. "Come on, Elaine," she said, "we're going in."

We marched to our pew single-file, and Johnny, who was an extremely friendly little boy and loved greetings, clattered rather more than was necessary and beamed all round him. He arranged his handkerchief, his prayer book and his penny in a careful row, and then collected three hassocks one on top of each other to make sure of seeing and being seen over the top of the pew when the congregation stood up. But after a certain amount of shoving and scuffling we all settled down, and the service began.

My thoughts wandered immediately, for I was not trying to listen. I kept repeating over to myself the words I had seen in the churchyard—"fulness of joy . . . fulness of joy."

I felt that these words were the heart of some tremendous secret, and perhaps the missing words were the key. In where, or in what, could fulness of joy be found? And what was fulness of joy? Nothing I had ever known in my dull, lonely little life, and yet something I was crying out to know. And as I stood there, forgetful of everything, but longing, something happened. The sun pierced the mists outside, and the church was suddenly filled with a golden glory, transfiguring the stained windows, streaming on the bright heads and snowy surplices of Peter and the other choir boys, making stars in Frances's wondering eyes and warming and blessing us all. Everyone lifted their faces in solemn amazement at this miracle of sunlight, and I glanced at Janet. She was standing with her head thrown back, singing at the top of her voice.

Just for a moment I thought I knew what fulness of joy must be like. It would transfigure everything, even the ugly things, and make all the dull, ordinary things precious and beautiful. But just as I made that discovery, a cloud blew across the sun, and the church was plunged into shadow again.

By the time we came out it was raining again, and we pranced home like young colts released from a stable. Cadwaller came bounding to meet us, behaving as though he, too, had had to sit still for an hour, and tried to leap up and greet us with his muddy paws on our Sunday coats, and we were all very warm and wet and rosy by the time we reached home.

After dinner it was still raining, so we gathered expectantly round the fire for Sunday toys. At a quarter past three we would go again to Sunday School, but before that a special cupboard was unlocked with books and puzzles and toys that only came out on Sundays, or if someone was ill. The box of chocolates I'd given them was produced too, and I was glad to see it, for at home my mother was always giving me sweets and chocolates, and I ate them whenever I liked. But here they seemed to appear only after Sunday dinner or round the fire after supper, and in consequence they were very exciting. In fact, Johnny had already started talking about them on the way home from Church.

It took a long time to decide who had what from the cupboard and a still longer time choosing choc-

olates, but at last an unusual quiet settled down
over the room. Peter and Janet were deep in books,
and Frances, who had given half her chocolate to
Cadwaller, was now reading him a story with her
arms round his neck. Johnny was making in plas-
ticine all the animals going into the Ark, and Robin
had toddled off to "help" his beloved Blodwen.
Mrs. Owen was upstairs with Lucy, and there was
no sound to be heard but the soft murmur of
Francie's voice and the munching of chocolates.

I was sitting at the table writing to Mummy,
but I couldn't think of much to say. "Dear
Mummy," I started, "please come and take me
home again. I don't like it here, and the children
don't want to play with me, and it's horribly cold
. . ." I sat biting my pen and gazing out into the
garden for further inspiration. The rain was still
falling, but it was a thin bright rain with the promise of sunshine behind it. And as I watched I suddenly noticed that the rain was not only bright,
but silver, and the drops on the hedges were
turning silver too, and I found that I was looking
at one of the brightest rainbows I'd ever seen in
my life. The children round the fire with their
backs to the window noticed nothing, and I did
not say anything. It was my rainbow, and I
wanted it to myself.

I had read stories about treasures hidden at the foot of the rainbow, and the foot of this rainbow was just up the hill. It seemed to touch the earth behind an old stone wall, and although I no longer believed in fairy stories and hidden treasure, I thought it would be fun to run and stand in the light with the colours breaking all over me.

I got up quietly, shut my writing pad and walked to the door. To my great relief no one asked me where I was going, for Peter and Janet were both absorbed readers, and anyhow they were not very interested in me. My coat was hanging in the hall and I slipped it on, turned the front door handle very softly, and escaped.

I trotted up the hill with the bright rain soft on my cheek, and the rainbow, which was paling a little now, still ahead. By the time I reached the wall where its foot had rested, it had disappeared altogether and the sun had come out.

I stood still looking up at the wall that had enclosed that enchanted spot, the foot of the rainbow. It had ivy hanging over it in curtains, and it looked secret and exciting. I followed it until it turned a corner, and then again round another corner, and this time I found a green wooden gate, and by glueing my eyes to the cracks in the boards I could see that those walls enclosed a little grey

stone house set in a garden, and the windows of
the house were all tight shut with dark blinds
drawn down over them.

I pressed down the latch of the gate very cautiously, but it was locked fast. The house seemed
quite empty, and perhaps no one lived here. The
garden where the rainbow had rested was a secret
deserted garden, and I suddenly wanted to get
inside it more than anything else in the world.

There were tall trees growing all round the inside of the wall with branches trailing over it. Peter
and Janet would have clambered over in a minute,
but to me it looked almost impossible. I wandered
along, searching for footholds, and very soon I
came to a hawthorn bush, behind which the wall
was broken down a little, and there were easy
footholds. I scrambled to the top quite easily,
swung on an apple bough which seemed stretched
out to welcome me, and landed with a squelch on
the muddy lawn. It was the first time in my life I
had ever attempted such gymnastics, and had
anyone been watching me I should not have dared
to try.

I stood very still, rather frightened by what I
had done and at first hardly daring to move. But
the voices of the birds encouraged me, for the garden was full of them, and the air was alive with

their singing. The flower-beds were choked with
weeds, but the snowdrops grew in clumps everywhere. It was an untidy garden covered with dead
leaves, and some of the plants had crumbling oak
leaves clinging round their stems, as though they
had pierced right through the middle of them.

I advanced a few cautious steps and examined
the house. Yes, it was quite empty. The windows
were all locked and darkened, and there were
great dusty cobwebs clinging across the front door.
I did not think anyone had lived there for a very
long time.

Then I turned to the garden again, wondering
just where the foot of the rainbow had rested,
and suddenly I knew—on a rising mound of lawn,
clear of leaves, there was a sprinkling of winter
aconites, still curled in tight balls, like babies
with golden heads and green Sunday collars.

I had often seen snowdrops on street barrows
and round the roots of trees in the parks, but I had
never seen these. I doubted if they grew anywhere
else in the world except in "my garden", and I
squatted there for a long time, with the pale January sun warming my damp hair and turning the
flowers to a brighter gold. Never, never had I been
in such a place; one particular scent was so sweet
and so strong that I got up after a time to try and

find out where it came from. It belonged to a bush of winter sweet growing up against the house.

Gradually I grew bolder, and then, forgetting fear altogether, I explored my kingdom from end to end. I decided to tell no one; I would come and play here all alone, and then it would not matter that I couldn't climb trees or play their silly games. And one thing I had discovered helped me a great deal. Lying against the back of the house was a half-rotten piece of ladder, which I dragged across the lawn and propped against the wall. It bore my light weight quite well, and I was able to get out of the garden quite easily.

I had no idea how long I'd been there, when at last I turned, nor what would be said about my absence, but the sky above the western hills was already brightening to sunset and the birds had nearly all stopped singing. Only a late blackbird, perched on an apple tree, carolled on.

"Fulness of joy," sang the blackbird, "fulness of joy . . . fulness of joy."

CHAPTER V

STIRRINGS UNDER THE SNOW

THE FAMILY HAD STARTED TEA when I got home, and Mr. Owen had gone out to look for me, but he saw me in the distance and came striding back. The children, as usual, were in a great state of excitement.

"Where have you been?" shouted Janet accusingly. "Daddy's gone to look for you, and you missed Sunday School."

"We thought you were drowned in the river," remarked Johnny cheerfully.

"Or stolen by gypsies," added Frances, her eyes very round.

"Or we thought perhaps you'd run away," chimed in Peter, his mouth full of cake.

"Where you BEEN?" demanded Robin, beaming at me over his mug of milk.

There was one good thing about these children; they asked questions so hard that there was never time to give an answer or explain, and I did not wish to explain. I looked rather anxiously at Mrs.

Owen to see if she was cross; she had certainly looked relieved when I came in.

"You musn't go so far alone till you know the way about, Elaine," she said gently. "The paths are muddling round here. Now stop asking where she's been, all of you; she doesn't know where she's been. She only came the day before yesterday."

Nevertheless, as soon as tea was over, she called me into the kitchen and, sitting down on a chair by the window, she drew me towards her and asked me herself where I'd been.

"Only for a walk," I replied rather rebelliously. "There's nothing wrong in going for a walk alone, is there, Mrs. Owen?"

"Oh, no," she said quietly, "there's nothing wrong at all. Janet often goes for walks alone. It's just that I'm afraid of your getting lost when you don't know the country. Come and tell me when you want to go out alone, Elaine, and then I shall know where you are."

I was rather surprised at this speech, for I had thought she was going to be cross, but she wasn't at all. Yet she seemed puzzled, as though she were trying to understand why I should want to be alone, and I had a sort of feeling that if I could make her understand, she would try and help.

"Mrs. Owen," I murmured confusedly, "do you see that wall?"

She gazed out into the dusk. Over the hills above "my cottage" there were still orange streaks in the stormy sky, and the wall was visible.

"Yes?" she answered questioningly.

"Well," I said, "I won't go any further than there—just round the other side of the bushes, there's a special place where I want to play. And please, Mrs. Owen, let me go and play there alone, and don't let the others come and look for me. I like playing alone better."

She smiled understandingly, for she knew all about special places. All her children had them. Peter and Janet had one together at the windy top of the beech, and Francie's was the animal cemetery, because she thought it was the gate of Heaven, and Johnny's was behind the rubbish heap. Even Robin had his own special place in moments of difficulty, underneath his mother's apron.

"You can play there whenever you like, dearie," she said kindly, "you've been used to playing alone, haven't you? All the same, I hope you'll sometimes play with Peter and Janet too. They'll like you to share their games."

I didn't answer and, having got what I wanted,

permission to play alone, I drew away. "I haven't finished my letter to Mummy," I said stiffly, and went back to the table, where I tore up my effort of the afternoon and started again. "Dear Mummy," I wrote, "I hope you are quite well. I like it in the country, and I should like to stay here a long time . . ."

I stopped writing; what would my garden look like after a long time? Perhaps it would grow into a garden like Mrs. Moody's, full of pansies and roses and lilies, and I would watch it unfolding all by myself. I forgot my letter and sat dreaming.

But it was a whole week before I went back to my garden, for next morning I started school, which took up most of my time and attention. I found the sturdy Welsh children different from my elegant little friends in London, and I kept myself to myself, although kind-hearted Janet did her best to look after me and drag me round with her. But Janet was extremely popular, and was always losing me and forgetting me in the eager crowd of merry girls of which she usually seemed to be the centre.

Besides, the mild misty weather was over, and by Tuesday there was a strange white light in the sky, and by Wednesday the snow had started to fall, and when we came out of school it was inches deep on the hills. The children went mad with joy, and all started snowballing each other. I got one right down my neck, and being unused to snowballing I lost my temper at once and got really angry. Janet, red in the face with shame, implored me in a frantic whisper to control myself, but the other girls giggled and drew away from me. "She's no sport," said one of them, and the game went on, but no one else threw snowballs at me. From that moment I was out of it.

Janet and I tramped up from the bus together in silence, miserable and shy of each other. As we reached the gate, Peter, who was home before us, burst out of the house.

"Come on, Jan," he shouted, "I'm going to help Mr. James bring in the sheep. I met him on the way up, and he says if we don't hurry some of the ewes will be snowed up in the ditches, and he thinks there's one going to have lambs to-night. Give your satchel to Elaine, and come quick!"

Janet, relieved to get away from me, swung her satchel on to my shoulder and dashed up the hill after Peter. They did not invite me to come too, I noticed, but actually I would not have wanted to, if they had, for my fingers and toes were numb with cold and my collar was wet from the snowball. I let myself in and went up to my bedroom, and sat down idly on my bed and stared out of the window.

Big snowflakes were floating down from a low grey sky, and the drifts were already piled against the wall of my garden. I began wondering what it looked like inside now. The snowdrops and aconites would be buried deep, and I wondered if they would die. And as I sat there hoping they would not, and gazing out into the white world, Mrs. Owen came in.

"Why, Elaine," she cried, "what are you sitting there for in your wet clothes? You must change your shoes and stockings and come down by the fire; you'll catch your death of cold sitting in this icy bedroom! Where's Janet?"

"Gone with Peter to bring in sheep," I answered absently. "Mrs. Owen, do flowers die when the snow buries them?"

She was already pulling off my stockings and chafing my numb feet with her strong, warm hands, and she laughed comfortably at my question. "Dear me, no," she answered. "There are wonderful things going on down under the snow. The flowers will close up, but the roots will be pushing down and drawing up water, and the bulbs and the buds will be storing up and getting fatter all the time. One day of sunshine will melt the snow, and the next will bring the flowers out in a rush."

I smiled in spite of myself, for I had a sudden vision of the roses and lilies pushing up so fast that I could see the petals unfolding. Besides, my toes were beginning to feel as though they belonged to me again, and up the stairs crept the delicious smell of hot toast. I felt comforted and went down to my tea with my hand in Mrs. Owen's.

The snow lasted for two more days, and Peter and Janet spent most of each evening up at the farm. On the second night, prompted by Mrs. Owen, they invited me to come too, and I went. Dusk had already fallen, and we all settled down in the barn where the ewes were brought when their lambs were born. One had had triplets that very morning, and Mr. Jones had been up most of the night with her. Now she lay peacefully on a heap of straw, her task triumphantly ended, and two tiny wrinkled lambs nuzzled her for milk.

"Where's the third?" asked Janet, squatting in the straw.

"Here," replied Mr. Jones with a chuckle, holding up a crumpled fleece. "'Twas born dead; I skinned it right away."

"What are you going to do with it?" asked Peter.

"Now you've just come in time to see," said Mr.

Jones, and he strode across the snowy yard with Peter and Janet at his heels, but I stayed where I was, seated comfortably on a chopping block watching the lambs and their tired mother, for I liked the barn, with its smell of sheep and leather and paraffin and straw. When we ran up the hill, the sky had been the colour of primroses and there were strange blue shadows over the snow, while the trees looked as though they'd been cut out of black paper and stuck against the sunset; but now the light had faded outside, and Mr. Jones had lit the lantern.

The lambs had finished feeding and lay curled as close as they could to their mother; it was a cold world to have tumbled into, and they were very small and crumpled. Outside a fox barked, and some weird night bird answered with its hunting cry, but the lambs only pressed a little closer against the sheltering flank of the ewe. Neither snow nor darkness nor night hunting could hurt them. They were safe and warm and satisfied.

I heard crunching footsteps in the snow outside, and Mr. Jones came in with the children behind him. In his arms he carried a third lamb, which snuggled against him as trustfully as the twins had snuggled against the ewe.

"Look, Elaine," whispered Janet eagerly, "it's an

orphan, its mother died. Mr. Jones is going to
dress it up in the fleece and see if this mother will
take it on."

It looked an absurd little object when the skin of
the dead lamb had been bound round it, and Mr.
Jones carried it up to the peaceful group in the
straw and laid it very gently against the flank of
the ewe. She turned her mild face to it and
sniffed it in a puzzled way, as though yearning for
her dead lamb. Then she laid her foreleg protect-
ingly over it and claimed it as her own; the queer
little creature snuffled and wriggled as though
pleading to be accepted, and then, quivering with
delight, pushed its head underneath her and
found its heart's desire.

But it had reckoned without its foster-brothers.
They turned angrily and started butting it with
their tiny heads, perhaps already feeling stubbly
horns stirring under their skin. And the frightened
little trespasser wriggled away crying and shivering and bleated aloud for a mother. Tender-
hearted Janet was down on the floor in a minute
gathering it into her arms, but Mr. Jones reached
out and took it from her.

"Now don't make a fuss of it," he said, "it's got to
make its way . . . I'll try again in half an hour's
time. It's bigger than those twins, and it must learn

to hold its own. Now you must be getting home, or your mother will be up to fetch you, indeed she will!"

We turned reluctantly from the warm, lantern-lit barn and went out into the clean frost. It was a starry night, and everything sparkled.

"Race me home," shouted Peter, setting off at breakneck speed down the crunching farm track with Janet at his heels. But I was afraid to run in the slippery frost and was just about to shout after them to stop and wait for me, for it was very unkind of them to dash off like that and leave me alone in the dark. If I shouted loud enough, Janet would come back and walk with me, for she was always kind if she remembered to be.

But suddenly I seemed to see that ridiculous dressed-up lamb crying for pity and to hear Mr. Jones's even voice as he picked it up: "It'll have to make its own way . . . it must learn to hold its own." It certainly did seem as though trying to make people sorry for you didn't get you far in the end.

I took a deep breath and began to run—cautiously at first, but I soon found that it was neither so difficult nor so dangerous as I had imagined. Clumsily and with a beating heart I began to gather speed, and as I galumphed along I passed the stone wall and thought of my buried garden with its stirring roots.

"There's wonderful things going on down under the snow," I murmured to myself.

CHAPTER VI

THE STRANGER IN THE GARDEN

ALL SATURDAY we tobogganed and snowballed and made a snowman with some of the village children, but by midday even I, so unused to the country, realised that a change was taking place. A south wind was blowing from the land, a warm, caressing wind, and by the end of the afternoon every tree was dripping, and the grass was showing through the toboggan tracks. The poor snowman was dwindling away in little rivers, and his hat had fallen down over his shoulders. By the light of an angry crimson sunset we squelched up to the farm in our wellington boots, and long before we reached the gate we could hear the restless cries of the folded lambs who smelt the Spring and were straining to gambol in the open meadows. "I'll let 'em out to-morrow," said Mr. Jones, who was sweeping out the barn. "Spring's on the way, and they know it!"

The children and Cadwaller knew it too, and

had seemed to me quite mad all day, rolling about in the snow in peals of senseless laughter or crazy barking, as the case might be—shouting, gambolling, pushing each other over. Fortunately they had not tried to push me over, and I had just stood about most of the time, feeling cold and bored. But I was glad to get back to the farm and the lantern light in the barn.

"What happened to the lamb, Mr. Jones?" I asked eagerly.

"Come and see," said Mr. Jones kindly, and we squelched through the muddy slush to the door of the fold. He held up the lantern and pointed to a corner.

"See there now," he exclaimed.

The ewe was lying on her side as before, and nuzzled against her were three lambs all feeding contentedly together. The biggest of the three seemed perfectly at home and even gave a little shove to the twin who was taking up the most room.

"What happened?" I asked. "Did they stop butting it?"

"No," chuckled Mr. Jones, "but she stopped crying and butted back; that settled 'em!"

He twinkled down at me, and I smiled up at him, and then we went bounding down hill again, hungry as hunters, and the orange lights in the windows shone out into the dusk to welcome us home. I was left far behind again, but instead of being angry my thoughts wandered to the sleeping garden. Perhaps even now snowdrops were pushing free to the call of spring, and the aconites were opening golden faces to the first stars. My heart beat fast with excitement, and I decided to go early next morning at the first streak of dawn, for we always had breakfast an hour later on Sunday, and there would be plenty of time.

Fortunately I woke very early, probably startled by the chorus of bird song that rose from the garden. The sky was a clear blue flecked with sunrise; little pink and golden clouds like curly feathers were scattered all over the East. Janet was fast asleep, and I dressed very softly and tiptoed downstairs; it was seven o'clock—two hours till breakfast.

There was a murmur of voices in the night nursery where the three youngest slept, and I paused for a moment on the stairs, wondering if Mrs. Owen was awake. But it was only Frances telling Robin, who had climbed into her bed, a Sunday story. I could see their fair heads close together on the pillow, and baby Lucy, still bright-eyed and solemn with sleep, gazed at them through the bars of her cot.

"God told Cain and Mabel to bring a lamb," said Francie's solemn voice, "but Cain brought vegubbles, but God didn't like vegubbles, and Cain gave Mabel a great big push and he fell down dead—and after that Cain was dreffully busy because he had to look after all Mabel's lambs as well as his own vegubbles."

Baby Lucy, feeling left out, pulled herself up by the cot rail and greeted the morning with a loud shout, which would probably rouse the house, so I sped on downstairs and slipped out through the front door—nor did I stop running till I was halfway up the hill; then I stopped to take breath and look round. A big thaw had set in during the night, and the air was mild and sweet. The snow lay deep in the ditches and in drifts in the fields, giving the land a striped appearance. But it was soft, wet snow, and the streams trickled down the paths. The earth was drinking deep, and I thought about the eager roots underground. "One day of sunshine, and everything will burst out"—that was what Mrs. Owen had said.

The sun was not yet up, but the sky grew brighter and clearer every moment, and perhaps the birds in the treetops could see it, for they seemed to be calling some joyful message to each other. But the garden, when I slipped over the wall and climbed down my ladder, was still asleep in the shadows, and the snow was piled against the house. But on the lawn it had melted, and the aconites smiled up at me, and the snowdrops clustered stronger and sturdier than ever. I wandered on enchanted and turned the corner. Then I stood quite still, rooted to the spot, for a man was standing in the little yard gazing at one of the darkened windows.

I do not know if I was frightened or just very astonished; I had not time to know anything before he glanced round furtively and saw me standing there. He gave a violent start, but seemed to recover himself at once, and walking up to me he said "Good Morning" in quite a pleasant voice.

"Is there anyone at home?" he asked rather uncertainly.

"I don't think so," I replied, "I think it's an empty house. Either no one lives here, or they've all gone away."

He frowned at me fiercely, and this time I definitely felt frightened. "Then what are you doing here?" he asked severely.

I might have said the same to him, but I did not think of it. I only minded about one thing, and that was that I should not be turned out of my garden, so I replied as boldly as I could, "Oh, I live just down the hill. I'm allowed to come here. I look after the garden."

He looked at me narrowly. "Thought you said you didn't know who lived here," he said after a moment's pause.

"Well," I answered, "I don't exactly know who they are, because I've only just come to live here, but Mrs. Owen down the hill knows them, and she said I could look after the garden."

I did not know whether Mrs Owen knew them or not, nor did I care, for no one had taught me the importance of speaking the truth. But once again the man's manner changed, and he spoke pleasantly.

"Well, it's a nice garden to mind," he said, looking round. "I'm a bit of a gardner myself. Would you be coming here every day?"

"Oh, no," I answered, "I go to school every day. I only come here on Saturdays and Sundays."

He looked relieved.

"Do you mean to tell me," he questioned, "that you see to this garden all alone? Would there be someone else now, who'd be coming in during the week?"

"I don't think so," I answered innocently, for I

did not like the idea of anyone else invading my secret place. But the moment I'd said it I wished I hadn't, for it began to dawn on me that this man had no business here, and why was he asking all those questions?

I did not like him; his face looked ill and haggared and unshaven, his clothes were dirty, and he smelt of drink. Nor did I like the way he kept glancing round out of the corner of his shifty, frightened eyes. I stared at him very hard, and I think he felt uncomfortable; suddenly pulling his cap down over his eyes, he turned away.

"Well," he said, "if the master's not at home, it's no use waiting. I'll call again. So long!"

He climbed the barred gate, vaulted over the top and was gone, and I gave a sigh of relief and turned back to my garden. But somehow the birds were no longer singing as they had sung before. Perhaps they had just been frightened away by our voices, but it seemed to me as though some evil shadow had fallen across the garden, and for the first time I felt lonely.

But not for long; as I stood wondering whether I should run home again, I saw a streak of golden brown, and a squirrel came darting down the trunk of an old chestnut in the corner. With one light leap he reached the ground and sat looking at me from between the roots of the tree. His bright eyes twinkled, and he twitched his tail impertinently, and all my loneliness melted away, forgotten. The garden was full of silent, satisfying company, and once again the birds had started singing.

I knew what I wanted to do that morning and I worked away happily until the sun came up over the hill. I wanted to make a little rockery like those I had sometimes seen in the parks behind railings—and then one day coming out of school, when Janet was busy with her friends, I would slip away unnoticed and buy seeds. Then when Summer came, my rockery would be a mass of fragrant colour, and the bees and butterflies would hum and flutter over it, just as they had done in Mrs. Moody's garden down in Sussex.

So I ran to and fro, banking up the soft earth and collecting stones till it was nearly breakfast time. And as I ran I noticed a ring of slender little shoots in the grass—dark green leaves guarding transparent sepals, and the crocus cups folded inside, waiting for the touch of the sun. Already I could see which would be purple, which would be orange, and which would be white.

"It's a fairy ring," I said to myself, for I had read about them, and here all by myself, with no one to laugh at me for being such a baby, it seemed easy to believe in such things, even though I was just eleven. I jumped into the middle of the ring.

"Now I can wish," I thought, laughing at myself and yet half believing, for the hidden place of tame squirrels and happy birds seemed so like fairyland. And I stood quite still, wondering what to wish for. "I know," I said to myself, "I'll wish for fulness of joy."

So I wished, and then, suddenly realising that it was time I went back to breakfast, I skipped out of the ring and down the hill with the wind blowing my hair out behind me. And as I ran, I heard strange cries above me, and looking up I saw the gulls wheeling and dipping with the sun on their wings. They had come in from the sea on the west wind to hunt in the softened spring fields.

On reaching the house I ran upstairs to tidy my hair, and found Janet kneeling by her bed, as she always did first thing in the morning and last thing at night, saying her prayers. I had noticed that when she rose from her knees she was usually in a specially good mood, so I thought I would take this opportunity to ask her a very important question. Also it might stop her from prying into where I'd been.

"Janet," I said, as she lifted her head, "do you know lots of texts in the Bible?"

"Oh, yes, nearly all," answered Janet airily. "Where have you been, Elaine?"

"Because," I went on, taking no notice of her question, "there's a special text, and I know the beginning and I know the end, but I want to know the middle. It's like this: 'In . . . something . . . is fulness of joy'."

"Well," said Janet cautiously, not wishing to own up to her ignorance, "I'm not quite certain, but I *think* it's 'in Heaven is fulness of joy'. In fact, I'm sure it is; I think I remember. There's the breakfast bell, come on!"

She danced away to help carry in the porridge bowls, but I stayed behind, slowly changing my shoes, for it always took some minutes for everyone to gather. I was disappointed in Janet's answer, for Heaven was far away, and I wasn't even sure that I'd ever get there. Mrs. Moody had told me that good people went there when they died, but I didn't know if I was good or not, and I'd never thought about it much. I thought I was better than Janet, for I didn't forget things, or lose my handkerchiefs as she did, nor was I so noisy and untidy. I went downstairs feeling rather self-satisfied; and yet, when I got there, I was not so sure. For it was Janet, not me, who had hurried down in time to help, and when Robin rushed in roaring, having fallen over in the yard, he ran straight past me into Janet's open arms.

Yes, there was no doubt about it, Janet cared about people in a way I did not. I had not realised that I cared for no one but myself, but I did wonder what made Janet different. I wandered upstairs after breakfast still thinking about it, and stood looking down curiously at the open Bible on her unmade bed, and the shabby little notebook inside it. What did she see in it, and what did she write down so carefully every morning? I stooped down to peep at what she had just copied out in her round, clear writing: "Be ye kind one to another, tender-hearted, forgiving one another, even as God for Christ's sake hath forgiven you."

CHAPTER VII

THROUGH THE OPEN WINDOW

We had a week of sunshine and west wind after the snow, and Spring arrived with a rush. Every day we hurried home from school, flung down our satchels, gobbled down our tea and went off up the hill. The evening air was tender with the cries of sheep and lambs, and deep in the larch woods we found the first primroses and white violets. Mrs. Owen had the utmost difficulty in making us do our homework.

The Owen children skipped and ran because they liked it, and I ran behind them because I had nothing else to do. Yet I was beginning to change. My garden had taught me the beauty and magic of this waking country, and scatter-brained little Janet, and even sturdy Peter, were beginning to teach me that life was more fun if you thought of other people as well as yourself; and going to Church and prayers at night were also teaching me something, but I wasn't yet quite sure what.

But I knew now that the Bible was not just a dreary book for dull grown-ups; it told of a Man in Whom I was beginning to be interested, a Man Who spent His life making sad people happy and naughty people good. Sometimes I wished I could come to Him, but I did not know how, and I was much too shy to ask.

And, perhaps strangest of all, I now really wanted to be one of them and no longer thought them stupid. Yet, although they tried to be patient, I knew quite well that they thought me stupid. My fears of cows, my slowness in climbing trees, my ignorance, and the time I took getting over a gate secretly astonished them, and sometimes I could see Peter jumping from one foot to another in his impatience at having to wait for me, and of course this made me slower and clumsier than ever.

As Spring drew on, and the primroses were no longer to be found singly but in wide-faced battalions, the children began to talk about birds, and John got out his collection of eggs and made new labels. In fact, we seemed to talk of nothing but curlews and moorhens and long-tailed tits and other creatures I'd never heard of, from morning till night. We roamed the country listening to I knew not what, for all the sweet notes which the

Owens could distinguish so easily sounded the same to me. They began to scale impossible trees, and we spent our free evenings in horrible prickly bushes and nettlebeds searching for nests. I dared not tell them that I had never yet seen a nest and knew no birds except sparrows. Their lives seemed dated by "the year we found the heron's nest at Anglesey", or "the Spring we found the gull's eggs on the Great Orme", until suddenly, about the end of March, there was a slight welcome variation.

Peter's form was taken for a day's coach outing to the Natural History Museum at Liverpool. It was pouring with rain when he returned, and we were indoors doing our homework or playing, while Mrs. Owen sat at her little desk doing accounts. Peter suddenly burst in on us, dripping and joyful.

"Mummy," he cried, "I've had such a smashing idea; I'm going to start a Natural History Museum here in the house!"

"Are you, darling?" said Mrs. Owen. "Four pounds of sugar . . . have you had a lovely time? . . . and have you changed your shoes?"

Peter flung his wet arms round his mother's neck. "Mummy," he shouted, "I'm serious! We should need a room and dozens of jam jars. Could we have the ones in the larder? And clear the loft?"

"But I need them for jam and bottling fruit," replied Mrs. Owen, smoothing her white collar. "And where should we put the things in the loft? Now change your shoes, and get out of that wet macintosh, and we'll talk about it at supper. We want to hear all about the Museum."

We did hear all about the Museum; we heard of nothing else and talked of nothing else for days and days and days, for Peter's enthusiasms were like measles, everyone caught them. We cleared all the lumber in the attic up to one end leaving half the room free, and Peter put up shelves. Then one rainy Saturday afternoon a Very Important Meeting was announced in the living-room, with Peter in the Chair, triumphant because he had just persuaded his mother to lend him the jam jars just till the jamming season began, rather to Blodwen's annoyance.

"If it's animals' insides and that sort of thing you're putting inside those jars, then I'm not using them for the preserves, DEFINITELY not," she remarked, suddenly sticking her head round the door, but no one took any notice of her. We were gazing at Peter, who was standing on a box, with an about-to-make-an-important-speech sort of look on his face, and his hand raised for silence.

"We shall have sections and departments in

this Museum," he announced grandly. "There'll be the birds' egg section, and the wild flower section, and the shell section, and the skeleton section . . . and . . . and . . . fossils and butterflies and anything else interesting anyone can collect."

"I'll collect rabbit holes," burst in Robin breathlessly. He had been trying to go down one that afternoon.

"We shall work in teams," went on Peter, waving his hand again for silence. "Two and two, and . . ."

"I'll go with you, Pete," yelled Johnny, flinging himself at the box and upsetting the speaker.

"Me and Jan!" shouted Frances, clutching her sister's skirt.

Peter and Janet looked at each other diplomatically. "If Elaine took the little ones, Jan and I might go together, and get a bit further afield," suggested Peter hopefully.

But the little ones burst into loud protests and I felt angry too. Nobody wanted me; the little ones wanted the big ones, and the big ones wanted each other. I flushed crimson with loneliness and hurt, and stalked to the door. "I'm not having anything to do with this silly old Museum," I shouted, "it's just a baby game . . . I'm sick of it. . . ."

I slammed the door behind me, and seizing up

my macintosh I ran into the garden. I heard
Janet come out and call after me, but I didn't
stop. Tears of anger and shame and self-pity were
running down my cheeks, and I wanted to get
away from them all. I hated them.

The rain had nearly stopped, and everything
smelt of wet earth and fresh growth. I had not
been to my garden for over a week—there was no
time with this silly bird craze—but I would go
now, quickly, before all the children came tumbling out of the house and saw me.

I was up the hill and over the wall in a few
minutes, and once again the peace of the place
seemed to cast a spell over me, and my stormy
little heart became quieter, for wonderful things
had happened in the garden. The almond tree
was jewelled with pink flowers, and the chestnut
tree on the lawn was holding up tiny leaves like
babies' hands. Round its roots the daffodils flow-
ered in a golden ring, and the birds still sang here
as they sang nowhere else. The seeds I had planted
on my rockery were beginning to sprout bravely,
and little honeysuckle tendrils swayed against the
stone walls.

I explored every nook and cranny. Tulip leaves
were pushing up in the beds, but of course I did
not know what all these things were at the time.

I stood looking at them wonderingly, and as I did so a brown bird with a white and speckled breast darted from the lilac bush beside me and made me jump. And then suddenly I drew in my breath, for the hours spent with Peter and Janet had taught me that birds darting out of bushes sometimes mount nests.

Surely it would never fall to my lot to find a nest of my own! With a hand that almost trembled I parted the boughs and peeped in. Yes, there *was* a nest, carefully woven from twigs and moss and mud, and down at the bottom of it lay two turquoise eggs speckled with black markings.

I looked and looked, holding my breath, my temper all forgotten. How could I have thought nests boring and stupid? Now that I found one myself, I knew they were the most precious, beautiful things in the world. Of course Peter and Janet would want to see it if I told them, but I wasn't going to tell them. It was my own secret, and I wasn't going to share it with anyone.

Then as I sat looking, I heard a cascade of song coming to me from the almond tree. The bird with the speckled breast was perched on the very top, brave and joyful against the sky and the soft light rain that had once more started to fall. I imagined it looked straight at me.

"It's our own secret," shouted the bird, "me and you . . . me and you . . . we'll keep it together . . . me and you . . . fulness of joy!"

I laughed outright, and then sat down quietly on a stone to await the bird's return. I rested my chin on my knees and stared at the daffodils and the clumps of primroses against the house. If only I could stay here for ever, where I felt good and happy! If only I had not got to go back to those hateful children who didn't want me! Tears of self-pity ran down my cheeks again at the thought of them, and I suddenly found myself longing for my mother—my pretty, careless mother, who had never seemed to want me very much either. In fact, no one really wanted me. All my life I should be lonely and unhappy, and I felt so terribly sorry for myself that I forgot all about the bird, and just stared in front of me; and then suddenly I noticed something so interesting that I even forgot to be sorry for myself and got up to investigate.

I ran towards the house to see better. No it was no trick of the light. One of those locked windows on the ground floor had been broken and opened and the curtains taken away. Where I had only peeped before, I could now look right in, and everything was different. The chest of drawers was open and things were spilt over the floor. It looked as though someone had been searching for something in a great hurry.

But what caught my attention most of all was something I had not been able to see when the curtains were drawn. It was a china cabinet in the corner full of beautiful shells; great cockle-shaped shells with strange horns, and shells like mother of pearl. I longed to see them more closely, and suddenly realised that there was nothing between me and them. The window was open at the bottom, and I only had to give a little jump and a pull, and I'd be inside. But what if anyone found me? That would never do. With a beating heart I tiptoed all round the house peeping into the other ground-floor windows. But they were all locked as before, with the blinds pulled down. Only the curtains from the kitchen window at the back were gone.

I tried the back door and the front door. They were locked, and cobwebs straggled across the cracks. No one had been in, and the gate was locked. I was safe to do as I pleased, and yet I did not feel safe. The garden suddenly seemed lonely.

With great caution and many backward glances I pulled myself up and planted my muddy shoes on the sill. Then I gave a jump and landed with a frightening thud on the boards, and picking myself up I tiptoed over to the glass cabinet and opened it. A sweet smell of old scented wood rose from it, and I stood fascinated in front of the shells.

I put out my hand and picked them up, one by one, and turned them over. They were rare foreign shells and corals, but I did not know that, and there was one not quite so big as the others, which seemed a different colour every way I turned it. In some lights it seemed silver, in some faint blue shot with a gleam of turquoise—then a twist of the hand, and it was pale grey with a glimmer of green. I laid it down almost reverently and tiptoed to the door, which I opened, and slipped into the dark passage. I stood listening for some time, then, getting bolder, I crept up the staircase.

I was going to explore!

CHAPTER VIII

THE RAINBOW SHELL

I PEEPED INTO THE FIRST BEDROOM and was amazed at its untidiness. A case was open in the middle of the floor with clothing hanging over the side, and again there were open drawers with the contents thrown about. Only the last bedroom I peeped into was in any sort of order, and that was a child's room, for the furniture was small and pretty, and there was a doll's house in the corner, and a family of dolls in a cot. I examined them with interest. Janet was not keen on dolls, and I had missed them. I wished Janet was the kind of little girl who played with dolls, for then we should have got on better. But this silly Museum . . .

Then suddenly the wickedness of what I was doing came over me, and I made for the door. I crept back into the room with the open window and stopped opposite the cabinet of shells. If only I could find a shell like the one with the colours for the Museum. Peter would think me cleverer than anyone and would never again call me stupid. Perhaps if I searched long enough on the beach I should find one, and yet we'd been down to the beach several times after school, and I'd never found one in the least like this.

And then suddenly a terrible thought came to me, because I was so unhappy and so longed to be admired. There were so many shells in the cabinet . . . if I just took that one and moved the others up a little, no one would know. And it wasn't really proper stealing, I told myself, because shells were free, anyone could pick them up on the beach. And then Peter would be sorry he'd said I was stupid, and Janet would think I was so clever. And no one could miss it or notice it, because it was an empty house anyhow.

For nearly five minutes I stood with the shell in my hand trying to persuade myself that it really could not matter. Then I slipped it into my pocket, crossed to the window and climbed out into the garden.

It was very still; that soft silver rain was still falling very gently, and the sky over the hills was saffron breaking through the grey. The flowers had closed their petals, and I almost imagined they were turning their faces from me. The birds had stopped singing. It was a sad twilight garden, and I wanted to escape and run home as fast as I could. I ran up the ladder and swung myself over into the wet grass, but when I picked myself up, I almost screamed. For Elwyn, the shepherd boy, was standing looking at me disapprovingly.

"What is it you are doing in that place, Elaine?" he asked slowly, for he was more accustomed to talking Welsh than English. "That is Mr. Thomas's house, and he did not say you could go in."

I was terrified; I felt as though Elwyn's round eyes were piercing holes in my pocket. I clutched the shell tightly and turned my scarlet face up to him.

"I'm . . . I'm allowed to," I faltered, I'm allowed to look after the garden, that's all. I never go to the house, only the garden . . . oh, please, Elwyn, don't tell . . . I'm allowed to!"

He stared at me. He was a dull, stupid boy and would probably have believed me if I had not looked quite so guilty. He shook his head slowly.

"Mr. Thomas he did say I was to keep an eye on the place," he remarked, "and you are not to go there any more, or it's Mrs. Owen I'll be telling of you. It is not the first time neither, I've seen you before."

"No, no," I cried, trembling, "I'll never go there

again, Elwyn. I only went in the garden." I ran past him down the hill with a beating heart, but before I'd reached the house I'd calmed down a bit. Elwyn was such a stupid boy, he'd be sure to forget all about it, and anyhow I'd told him I'd only been in the garden. There were dozens of shells, and no one would notice one. I would not dare go back and play in the garden for a time, but somehow I did not mind that, for the garden I had loved so dearly, that had been to me such a sanctuary of peace, had suddenly become strange and frightening.

I stopped and stood still to think. I had to decide what I would do about the shell. It was no good giving it to them tonight, as they would know I hadn't been on the beach. I would wait till after school on Monday, and slip down to the shore when Janet was chattering to her friends. I would come home later, alone, with my pockets full of shells as a gift for the Museum, and the rest was easy. So I pretended to be in a very good mood when I sauntered rather self-consciously into the house, and Janet, who was always quick to make up a quarrel, came running up to me and begged me to come with her and Peter next day. I nodded coldly and said that I had ideas of my own and would probably go alone, which rather took her aback.

But I was very silent at supper, and Mrs. Owen glanced once or twice at my pale, troubled face, and when Peter bounced out of his seat and opened the Bible in front of his father, I felt as though I wanted to run away. I was beginning to get quite interested in the Bible, but to-night I did not want to listen.

"Let me see," said Mr. Owen, "where did we get up to? It was Genesis 3 last night."

"We got up to where Adam and Eve stole the apple," said Janet eagerly, "and they hid from God."

"Ah, yes," replied her father, and he read on in his beautiful voice that made the story live—a sad, sad story of a man and a woman sent out of a beautiful garden where they had been so happy, to sorrow and weariness and death—and all because they did wrong. Why had they been so happy in the garden? Because God was with them; but sin separated them from God, and then there was nothing but sadness. Very simply Mr. Owen explained it, and the children sat with their grave young faces cupped in their hands, their eyes fixed on their father. But I sat looking at my plate, half listening and half lost in my own thoughts, and after prayers were over, I said I had a headache and asked if I might go to bed.

Mrs. Owen came upstairs when I was in bed and took my temperature and gave me an aspirin. She stayed with me talking to me in her kind motherly voice as though I'd been her own child, and I had a great longing to fling my arms round her neck and tell her all about everything, but of course if she knew I was a thief she wouldn't love me any more, and she might send me away. So I just lay still and let her talk, and when she kissed me goodnight I half turned my head away, and she went downstairs, puzzled and sad.

But I lay awake in the dark thinking about the story and in my drowsy mind I thought it must have been written about me. "The Lord God sent him forth from the garden," and I knew that even if I got past Elwyn, which I dared not do, the garden would never again be beautiful and happy and peaceful because of what I had done. Perhaps, somehow, God had been waiting for me among the Spring flowers, waiting to make me happy, like Adam and Eve, but my sin had spoiled it all. And then I remembered something else—I should never see the eggs hatch, nor would the thrush share her secrets with me any longer. The pale points would spring up, and the feathery plants on the rockery would grow sturdy under April suns and rains, but I should be outside. I buried my face in the pillow and wept, but when Janet came up, I pretended to be asleep.

Next morning the sun was shining, and I felt better, and all Sunday I tried to be very good and helpful to make up for the night before, while on Monday morning I was ready before Janet to help with the little ones. Lucy was bouncing up and down in her cot waiting to be dressed.

"'appy! 'appy!" shouted Lucy at the top of her voice, shaking the bars, and I lifted her gingerly on to the floor. It was quite easy to get her nightgown off, but impossible to get her petticoat on. She clenched her fists and went quite stiff, and when I coaxed her, she lay flat on the floor and kicked. The crosser I got, the more she giggled and gurgled, until I became exasperated and slapped her. Her mouth went down at the corners, and she opened it to roar, when all of a sudden she shut it again, and a light of joy broke over her fat face. She struggled to her feet and staggered to the door, beaming through her tears.

"Dan, Dan, Dan!" she shouted, flinging herself into Janet's arms and clinging to her for dear life.

"You mustn't slap Lucy," said Janet indignantly, slipping her clothes on without the slightest difficulty, "she's only a baby. Besides, she'll catch cold if you let her lie on the floor with nothing on. You really don't know much about babies, Elaine."

I didn't, and I didn't want to. I went down to breakfast hating all babies from the bottom of my heart. They were so unreasonable and awkward and sticky and noisy, I thought, looking disgustedly at Robin, who seemed to be spreading himself with marmalade. Lucy was banging her spoon against her high chair till we could hardly hear ourselves speak. I wondered how Mrs. Owen bore with them. I was glad to get off to school and leave them to their rampagings, but school wasn't very successful either. I felt restless, frightened, and unsettled, and even got my first bad mark for inattention. Janet, trying to convey her sympathy, spent so much time screwing her head round to look at me that she finished up by getting one too. I felt this was rather kind of her, and I would have liked to join her after school and bicycle home with her, but my business had to be done, and the moment we were let out I slipped away from the noisy group that always gathered round Janet, and made for the beach.

It was not a very good place for shells, but I collected a few ordinary ones and put them into

my pocket with my treasure. Then I drew it out
and held it in the sun. It looked lavender-coloured,
but when I tilted it towards the sea, it turned
green, and once again I thought it was the most
beautiful thing I'd ever seen, but I did not want
to stop and think about it. I ran up the pebbles
and pedalled after Janet, who had already started
home.

"Where've you been?" asked Janet.

"Down to the beach," I answered rather breathlessly. "I've got some shells for the Museum, and I
found one beauty. I've never seen one like it before."

"Show me," said Janet, putting on her brake.

I shook my head and pedalled on. "When we get
back home," I called, "I'll show you and Peter together."

We raced rather recklessly along the main road
and turned up the lane that led to the Vicarage
where emerald larch trees grew on the banks and
the soft air smelt of primroses. Janet's nose quiv-
ered like a rabbit's, and she began to sing with joy
at the prospect of getting home. But I pedalled
along behind her, silent and nervous.

Peter was home already, for his school was a little nearer. He was engrossed in making a new box
for his birds' eggs and only grunted as we came in.

"Come on, Elaine, show us!" said Janet eagerly. "Peter, she says she's found a very special rare shell on the beach. Bring it out, Elaine."

"That beach is no good for shells," answered Peter, barely looking up, "you have to go a long way further on . . . oh, crumbs! I say, Elaine, you didn't really find that one on our beach, did you"

"I did," I answered defiantly, "if you don't believe me, ask Janet. She knows I went down after school."

"All right, keep your hair on," retorted Peter, glancing at me in some surprise. "Nobody said you didn't, only it's a queer thing. It must have been washed miles and miles from some other coast. We must have a very special place for it in the Museum. Jolly good show, Elaine!"

Janet was holding it in her hands, turning it round and round to the light. The little ones gathered round, standing on tiptoe to see.

"It's like Philippa's shells in the cabinet," said Janet wonderingly. "It's beautiful, Elaine, first it's pink, now it's blue, now it's mauve! We must show Daddy."

They burst into Mr. Owen's study, where he happened to be writing letters, but I hung back uneasily. I'd often head them speak of Philippa. She was a child from the village, who had had polio, and she'd been in a hospital all the Winter. But where did she live, and when was she coming back?

Mr. Owen turned to me over the heads of his excited children. "You found this on the beach, Elaine?" he asked in a puzzled voice. "It's a most extraordinary find. It looks like real mother-of-pearl. Either someone dropped it, or it's been washed by the tide right across the world. It's nice of you to lend such a treasure to the Museum."

"Yes, thanks awfully, Elaine," said Peter in a hurry, lest it might occur to me to keep it. "It really is awfully decent of you . . . we'll go and see where we can put it. It's our star exhibit."

They tumbled through the door and up the staircase to the loft. Mrs. Owen smiled kindly at me, and I gave her a wan little smile. Then, instead of going with the others, I followed her into the kitchen.

"Auntie," I asked, "where does Philippa live?"

"Why, at the cottage just up the hill," answered Mrs. Owen. "We're hoping she'll be back soon. I heard from her mother that she was better."

I turned away and went out into the garden, and Cadwaller trotted up to me and rubbed his kind old head against my legs, as though he smelt that I was in trouble. I knelt down on the path and buried my face in his shaggy coat and flung my arms round his neck, for Cadwaller didn't care what I'd done. I might have stolen and told lies and all the rest of it, but to Cadwaller I was just an unhappy little girl needing comfort. He put out his tongue and licked me.

CHAPTER IX

WHAT HAPPENED IN THE BEECH WOOD

EXAMS WERE OVER, and we woke up one rainy morning to the first day of the Easter holidays. Everyone was full of outdoor plans, but an absolute downpour at breakfast put an end to them, and we all settled down to a day at home. Mrs. Owen produced jobs for the older members of the family that kept us busy for some time. Janet and I polished silver at the kitchen table, while Peter sat on some newspapers at our feet cleaning shoes, and we chattered and sung and made more plans. Mrs. Owen was with Blodwen doing the washing at a tub at the sink and told us funny stories of when she was a little girl, and the little ones tumbled about with Cadwaller. At eleven, work was over, and we all gathered for hot cocoa and biscuits.

Peter was making a large map of the district to hang at the back of the Museum with such labels as "Moorhen's nest Pond" . . . "Butterfly orchids grow here" . . . "Red spotted toadstools here" . . . "Owl's nest three years running in this oak." He liked to work at it all spread out on the floor, but Lucy always seemed to think it was a sort of pedestrian crossing that she must stagger across at all costs, and someone had to go on duty at each end to ward her off. She was particularly determined that morning and kept charging dangerously at the ink.

"I say," said Peter, lifting a flushed face from his work, "I suppose one of you girls wouldn't do something about old Lucy, would you? No, baby dear, you *can't* . . . oh, I say, look! There's a Bobby coming up to our front door! I wonder what he wants. Perhaps Cadwaller has killed another hen . . . quick, Cadwaller! Hide—good dog!"

Everyone, including Cadwaller, had crowded to the window to look at the policeman, so mercifully no one was looking at me; for I had suddenly gone very white and cold, and there was a queer sick feeling inside me. Just supposing it wasn't Cadwaller, just supposing they had found out something, and it was me they were after? Just supposing Philippa had come back and noticed that her shell was missing, and Elwyn Jones had said something? I stopped supposing, and just slipped into the kitchen and out of the back door. Whatever it was all about, I felt safer out of the way.

"Where are you going without your macintosh, Elaine?" called Blodwen from the sink, but I took no notice. All the fears hidden away in my heart for nearly a week now were rising up in front of me. I ran up the hill as fast as my trembling little legs would carry me, and I did not know where I was going, but I kept clear of Philippa's house. I took the upper path that ran across the sheep pastures and the fat April lambs gambolled away in front of me. I forgot that on the high path I could be seen from the windows of Mr. Owen's study.

I had reached the level highlands above the farm, and it had stopped raining. Over the hills stretched a washed turquoise sky, and wherever I looked there were hills and valleys and steep sheep-dotted fields. Away to the south towards the great mountains the sun was shining, and I could see the purple crests of the Snowdon range. But even in my panic I knew that I could not reach those great rocks. I must find a nearer hiding-place than that, and I looked round furtively. To my right was a wood where we were not allowed to go, for it was a pheasant preserve. But nothing mattered now; if the Police were after me in any case, it did not matter if I was trespassing or not.

I slipped between the bars of the padlocked gate, for I was a little, thin girl for eleven, and I trotted along the path too out of breath to run any more. In spite of my fright I could not help noticing what a beautiful wood it was. The smooth grey beeches were bursting into tiny leaves like pale green feathers, and the ground was starred with anemones and primroses. Bluebell leaves were piercing the old russet of last year's fall, and once I saw a glint of gold in a bog where the kingcups were out. Once a fine cock pheasant started up with a loud whirr at my feet and gave me an awful fright, but mostly the air was full of gentle sounds—the distant bleating of lambs, the murmur of wood pigeons, the flurry of busy little wings and the soft chirpings of birds building nests. Arched boughs met overhead, and it felt almost like being in church.

I reached a little clearing in the heart of the wood, where someone had made a pile of logs, and here I sat down and tried to think. If I went too far, I knew I should come out on the road again, and that I did not want to do. But what was going to happen next I did not know, for the more I thought about it, the more I felt I could not go back

Back, to face the policeman and the shocked faces of Peter and Janet who never told lies? I couldn't do it! They would think me so wicked and so terribly silly, and anyhow, what would the policeman do? I did not know whether they sent children of my age to prison or not, but I was sure they did something to them . . . and what would my mother say? And Mrs. Moody?

I sat there on the logs for a long time. It must have been long past the dinner hour, but I was not hungry. I sat so still in my fear and grief that a squirrel began to play on the tree in front of me, leaping from branch to branch. A bright-eyed baby rabbit lolloped through the bluebell leaves, and the birds on busy errands darted to and fro. Everything seemed happy and busy and fearless except me.

One thing I noticed, and never forgot. It was the beauty of a little clump of wood sorrel springing out of a piece of rotten bark beside me. Never had I seen greener leaves or frailer white flowers. I broke off the piece of bark and held the whole clump in my hand like a tiny fairy garden; and then suddenly the silence was broken by the bark of a dog and the sound of quick, steady footsteps coming through the forest.

The police! I seemed to freeze with fear. Perhaps they were hunting me with bloodhounds and police dogs; I had read about them once in a comic. I think I gave a little scream, for there was a loud answering bark of joy, and Cadwaller leaped through the trees and put his paws on my shoulders and began licking my face in an ecstasy of welcome, and behind him came Mr. Owen. I looked up at him, gave a great sigh of relief, and burst into a flood of tears.

He sat down beside me on the log and put his arm round me and quieted me as though I had been Janet. When at last I was able to control myself, he said very gently, "Why did you run away, Elaine? Were you frightened of that policeman?"

So he did know, and they were looking for me, and the sooner I got it off my chest, the better. And somehow, with Cadwaller pressed against my legs and that strong, kind arm holding me, I felt that after all it might be possible to face the consequences and go on living. I nodded and sniffed.

"But why were you afraid, Elaine?" asked Mr. Owen. "He only wanted to ask you a few questions. But I will ask you instead, and then to-morrow we'll go and tell him the answers."

"What will he do to me?" I whispered.

"Why, nothing, Elaine," he answered in a puz-zled voice. "I don't suppose you've done any-thing wrong. Only, you see, there's been a robbery in Mr. Thomas's house, and Elwyn Jones says you've been playing in that garden, and the Police wanted to ask you whether you'd seen anyone about, and whether you'd noticed how long ago the window was forced open, and also whether you'd ever been into the house, because there were little muddy footprints on the sill that belonged to a child."

I sat very still, my mind in a whirl. Was I the robber or was there someone else as well? Who had opened the window and searched the drawers? Not me, or did they perhaps think it was me?

"Tell me about it," said Mr. Owen at last.

The wood seemed very still, as though all the birds and flowers were holding their breath, lis-tening for my answers.

"I didn't open the window," I blurted out. "Truthfully I didn't. I just went in to look at the shells—and I just took one—I thought shells didn't matter much, because they were free and you picked them up for nothing—and they all said

I was so stupid—and no one wanted to go with me—and I always get left behind—and I don't know anything about birds, and I thought they'd like me if I found a shell, so I said I'd found it on the beach. And Peter was so pleased—and they'll think I'm awful now—and I didn't know it belonged to Philippa—"

I trailed off miserably. It was all out, and what would happen now I couldn't imagine, and yet strange to say my heart felt lighter.

"Please, please, Mr. Owen, don't make me go back to the Police," I whispered. "Make Mummy come and take me home. I'm so miserable, and now it will all be worse."

I looked up at him timidly, pleading. He was looking rather sad.

"You needn't be so afraid, Elaine," he said gently. "The Police didn't come to ask about the shell. They don't know about it, nor need they ever know about it. It was quite a big robbery—blankets and curtains and silver and all sorts of things. It wasn't anything to do with you. They only thought you might have seen someone hanging round the house and be able to explain about those little footmarks. There is nothing to be frightened of at all. You and I can deal with that shell between us."

"There was a man," I murmured, "once, early in the morning, looking in at the window."

"Well then, you'll be able to help the Police a lot," said Mr. Owen encouragingly. "Peter will be quite jealous of your having seen a real burglar. We'll go to the Police Station to-morrow, you and I, and you must tell them what the man looked like, that's all. Now let's forget about that, and let's talk about the shell. You took it because you wanted them to think that you'd found something nice for the Museum, and you said you'd found it on the beach?"

"Yes," I whispered.

There was a little silence. "Did it make you happy?" asked Mr. Owen at last.

I shook my head. "I kept being afraid you'd find out," I said.

"That wasn't the only reason you were unhappy," said Mr. Owen. "You were unhappy because you'd stolen and told a lie. Sin always makes us so unhappy. Don't you remember the story we read the other night at prayers, about Adam and Eve?"

"Yes," I answered rather vaguely, "they were in a beautiful garden too; but I only went there to make it grow. I didn't mean to be naughty at first —there were snowdrops, and it was all quiet and beautiful and the birds sang—I didn't even pick flowers."

"Of course not," said Mr. Owen. "Mr. Thomas wouldn't have minded your playing in his garden at all. You loved it, and you were happy until you took that shell, just as Adam and Eve were happy until they disobeyed. And why do you think they were so unhappy then?"

"'Well, they were frightened," I answered.

"Yes, they were frightened," agreed Mr. Owen. "And far worse than that, their sin had come between them and God, just as a cloud comes between us and the sun. The sun is still there, but we can't enjoy it. The cloud has blotted it out, and everything is cold and dark. And there is only one place in the world where we can find real happiness, what the Bible calls 'fulness of joy'."

I quite jumped at hearing the familiar words and I looked up quickly. "I know that text," I whispered, "Janet taught it me—'In Heaven is fulness of joy'."

Mr. Owen laughed. "Then Janet taught it you all wrong," he replied. "It's far, far better than that. It's like this: 'Thou wilt show me the path of life; in Thy presence is fulness of joy.' That means that anywhere in the world, here in this wood or at home in the Vicarage, if you are walking along the path of life close to God you can be perfectly happy. And sin is the only thing that separates you from God. Only find out how sin can be taken away, and you'll know the secret of fulness of joy."

I sat very still, for I felt I was on the verge of a great discovery. I even forgot my misery for a few minutes.

"How?" I asked.

"It's a long, long story, Elaine," said Mr. Owen, "and it's the most beautiful story in the world. It was just to take away our sin that Jesus came to this earth as a man. When He hung on the Cross, He took that sin that was between us and God and was punished for it instead of us. It says in the Bible, 'He took it out of the way, nailing it to His Cross'. And if there is something between two people and someone comes and takes it away, what is left?"

"Nothing," I said.

"Nothing between," said Mr. Owen, "just an open way for sinners to come to God, because Jesus died. Nothing to stop you any more. You can come right into His Presence and find fulness of joy."

My eyes were fixed on his face. What did it mean? What had I got to do next?

But I could not ask these questions aloud, I

could only wonder. Cadwaller had laid his head on my knee, and I fingered his silky ears in silence. The golden stillness of evening seemed to have fallen over the wood. Mr. Owen pulled his Testament out of his pocket and opened it at the first chapter of John's first Epistle.

"Do you want to hear how sin can be taken right away?" he asked. "It's all here, written down for you."

I sniffed and nodded. I wanted to know so badly, but I still couldn't say anything.

So he read them aloud slowly, and I leaned against him and read them too—the verses I was to love so much later on, those verses written by an old man whose eyes had actually once seen his Saviour hanging on the Cross.

"These things write we unto you, that your joy may be full . . . if we walk in the light, as He is in the light, we have fellowship one with another, and the blood of Jesus Christ His Son cleanseth us from all sin. If we say that we have no sin, we deceive ourselves, and the truth is not in us. If we confess our sins, He is faithful and just to forgive us our sins, and to cleanse us from all unrighteousness."

CHAPTER X

INTO THE LIGHT

WHAT DOES 'CONFESS' MEAN?" asked Mr. Owen.

"Saying you did it," I whispered shamefacedly.

"Yes, that's right," he answered, "it's telling God about the sins you can remember and asking Him to take into account all you can't remember and then believing that He laid them all on the Cross of Jesus and they were all paid for there. And then, because there is nothing between you any more, you can come straight to God and give yourself to Him to obey and serve Him for ever. Would you like to do it?"

I nodded again.

"Then tell Him about it now," said Mr. Owen. "Tell Him what you did, tell Him that you believe that Jesus has died so that it can be forgiven, and then thank Him for making you clean and leading you into the light."

"I don't know what to say," I whispered.

"Then I will pray," said Mr. Owen, "and you can say it with me in your heart." So we closed our eyes, and he prayed out loud: "Oh, dear Lord, I want to tell you about the shell I stole and the lies I told and all the things I was so afraid and unhappy about. I am coming to You because Jesus died and You promised to forgive. Please wash me whiter than snow and make me Your own little girl. And come into my heart and make me brave and truthful, so that I can put right what I did. For Jesus' sake, Amen."

I opened my eyes and looked round half expecting to see some visible Presence standing near. The wood was all aglow with sunset as we rose to our feet and set off home hand in hand with Cadwaller bounding ahead on the scent of private rabbits. As we reached the white gate, every far peak stood out separate and shining, revealed in the last light, and the clouds were flung like bright banners across the West.

"Walking in the light," I thought to myself, "that's what it's like—all gold with nothing hidden," and I suddenly felt brave and strong and joyful for a few minutes. But it didn't last, for, as we crossed the uplands, the Vicarage came into sight below us, with Peter and Janet waiting for our return, and I knew what my new Master was telling me to do. If only Mr. Owen would not walk so fast. I hung back, and he looked down at me.

"What are you thinking about?" he asked. "Are you afraid?"

I nodded dumbly.

"Then you know what you've got to do to put it right?"

I nodded again.

He gave a little smile and held my hand very tightly.

"Let's tell them about it together after tea," he said reassuringly. "You'll be so much happier when it's all over, and you can start again; and anyhow it won't be as bad as you think. Peter and Janet have got a lot to put right, too, as far as I can see."

The light had faded as we passed my garden, and the dusk had fallen. Along the ridge above the path came Mr. Jones with his flock in front of him. In his arms he carried a lamb; I wondered why. Perhaps it was tired or lame, or perhaps it couldn't keep up with the others. Anyhow, it would get home safely in the shepherd's strong, kind arms. Then I forgot about it, for my thoughts were all in a turmoil, and I was feeling more frightened than I had ever been before in my life.

The children looked at me curiously when I came in, but asked no questions, for Mrs. Owen had told them not to, and tea would have been a silent, uncomfortable meal if Mr. Owen had not announced that I had almost certainly seen the burglar who had broken into Philippa's house, and to my surprise I suddenly found myself the heroine of the hour. Everyone wanted to know what he looked like, and Peter started launching complicated plans for catching him ourselves. We went on talking about it again after prayers, and everyone looked surprised when Mr. Owen called from his study that he wanted to see Peter and Janet and me.

He was sitting back in his easy chair, and Peter and Janet hurried forward and sat down, one on the arm and one on the rug at his feet. But he pushed them away a little and made room for me, as I hung back silent and afraid in the doorway. And when I too was curled up on the rug and leaning against his knees, he said quietly, "Elaine wants to tell you something."

There was nothing for it. With a bent head I blurted out my little story.

"It was the shell . . . I didn't find it . . . it was Philippa's . . . I wanted something for the Museum . . . it wasn't true . . ." and burying my crimson face against Mr. Owen's legs, I burst into bitter tears.

"Just a minute, Elaine," said Mr. Owen, "You

haven't quite finished. Why are you telling us about it and putting it all right?"

"Because," I sobbed, "I asked God to forgive me in the wood, and I want to start again."

"Good," said Mr. Owen. "Now you've obeyed the Lord Jesus to Whom you gave yourself this afternoon, and you need not be unhappy any more. We are not going to punish you, because you are sorry without any punishment. You can go now, and start all over again, but . . ." and here his voice suddenly changed and became rather stern, "I want you, Peter and Janet, to stay with me. I want to tell you just why Elaine took that shell."

I crept away, not daring to look up. To my relief the little ones had gone to bed, but Mrs. Owen was sitting darning by the fire. She smiled at me, and I sat down close beside her, too exhausted to speak, but longing for her kind, motherly company. Perhaps Mr. Owen had already told her all about it, for she asked no questions. She just began talking about all the fun we were going to have in the Easter holidays. I should have liked to stay beside her, but I did not want to be there when Peter and Janet came out of the study. I could just imagine the clear contempt in Peter's honest blue eyes and Janet's expression of mixed pity and dislike. So after about five minutes I went up to bed, and Mrs. Owen came up a little later and tucked me in and kissed me goodnight.

It seemed a long time before Janet crept softly into the room and started undressing without turning the light on. I shrank down under the bedclothes pretending to be asleep, but I think she must have known I was pretending, for she suddenly flung herself down beside me.

"Elaine," she whispered, "don't be asleep! Listen! Pete and I are most awfully sorry, honestly we are."

"Whatever for?" I asked, coming up from my burrow in astonishment. This was not at all what I had expected.

"Because Daddy said it was partly our fault that you took that shell," said Janet, her words all tumbling over each other in her earnestness. "He said it was all because we were selfish and only wanted each other and didn't want to share. And he read us an awful story in the Bible, and I cried ever so, and I think even Pete did a bit, too."

"What awful story?" I asked, much interested.

"Oh, a story about some people who were unkind and selfish, and Jesus said to them, 'I was hungry, and you wouldn't give Me anything to eat, and I was once a stranger, and you wouldn't share and play with Me.' And when they said they'd never seen Jesus before, Jesus said, 'It was when you wouldn't share and play with My little ones.' I'll show it to you in the morning. It's in Matthew 25. Daddy said it was like us, and you were the stranger, but really it was Jesus all the time."

Her voice broke, and she sniffed. I crept closer to her.

"It's not true," I whispered. "You often tried, but I was so cross, and sometimes I didn't want to be friends. And I know it was terribly wicked of me to take that shell and say I'd found it on the beach. I can't think how I did it—I just thought—I wanted you to like me."

"But we do like you," cried Janet, raising her hot little face, "and we think it was jolly brave of you to tell, and we want to be friends and share, dreadfully badly now."

"And I'm not going to be cross any more," I whispered, "because, you see—of what happened this afternoon. I expect I shall get nicer now.

"I know," said Janet eagerly. "I'm ever so glad about that part because, you see, I belong to Jesus, and so does Pete, and lots of times we've wanted to tell you, but we thought you'd think us so silly, and Daddy says it wouldn't have been much good telling you either, because we were so selfish. But now we'll both be Christians together, and it will be super fun!"

"Could I read the Bible with you in the mornings?" I asked anxiously. "You see, I don't know my way about like you do, and you could show me."

"I think it would be wizard," said Janet, whose spirits were rising fast, and we pushed our beds close together and lay talking until her eyes closed and she fell asleep in the middle of a sentence. But I lay on wide awake, thinking back over that strange, stormy, terrifying, wonderful day. Yet here was I, at the end of it, lying at peace with all the world, unafraid and forgiven, with kind, thoughtless, eager little Janet lying close beside me, friends at last! And then I suddenly remembered Mr. Jones striding along the stormy ridge with the lamb in his arms, and I smiled a little. I was like that lamb, unable to go any further, but Jesus had come and lifted me up and brought me through. He had been with me all the time and would stay with me for ever, and in His Presence was comfort and peace and fulness of joy.

CHAPTER XI

"WALKING IN WHITE"

I T CERTAINLY DID SEEM as though life had started again. I shall never forget the feeling that came over me when I woke up next morning, and knew that I had left my dark secret behind me for ever and was no longer going to stumble fearfully on alone. I belonged to Jesus, and He would show me the path of life, and I should know all about fulness of joy if I walked with Him. That was what Mr. Owen had said to me, and the very birds seemd to shout it out on the pink apple trees and the feathery beeches. Never before had the sky seemcd so bluc or thc daffodils so goldcn. I leaned far out of the window in my nightgown, sniffing the dawn and longing to wake Janet. But she was fast asleep, so I crept back into bed and fell asleep again too from sheer joyful relief.

There was still Peter to be faced, but although he couldn't say it I knew that he was sorry, and all day long in his shy, gruff way he was trying to show me that they wanted to share. Besides, he was still frightfully excited about the burglar, and when that afternoon I actually had to go to the Police Station and describe the man I'd seen, his envy and admiration knew no bounds. He was still quite sure we could catch the man ourselves, and was for ever making me crouch in bushes to watch passers-by, or prowl behind innocent farm labourers. I was flattered by being so important, but I got rather tired of it and felt glad when he began to give it up as a bad job.

My great joy those holidays was the morning time with Janet, when we read the Bible together and chose and copied out the verse that became a sort of part of our day. Janet had so got into the habit of keeping this quiet ten minutes before breakfast that she would no more have missed it than her porridge, and I quickly realised that in order to walk close to Jesus, sharing His fulness of joy, you have to come into His Presence every morning and listen to His Voice speaking through the Bible.

It was on the first Sunday after that never-to-be-forgotten day that Mr. Owen called me into his study just before Church and gave me a parcel. When I had unwrapped it, full of excited curiosity, I found a beautiful navy-blue leather Bible with gold-edged pages and pictures, and when I opened it, too pleased to speak, I found my own name written on the front page and my own verse:

ELAINE NELSON

"Thou wilt show me the path of life.
In Thy Presence is fulness of joy."

I loved my Bible better than anything else I possessed, although as yet I knew very little about it. But we read notes that explained the passages, and Janet was always ready to add explanations of her own. I don't know how right they were, but they satisfied us both completely, and I think she enjoyed our readings as much as I did.

We did not always stay up in the bedroom. Some mornings we ran out into the garden and sat under the apple trees with the pink petals drifting down on to our hair and open books. Sometimes we climbed the moundy, hummocky meadows where cowslips grew in the hollows half as high as my knees. But on Easter Sunday we woke very early and found the world absolutely radiant with light and song and colour. So we picked up our books, and without speaking to each other, because we both knew where we wanted to go, we set off, running across the silver grass to the bluebell spinney.

Bluebell Spinney was a sloping wood of young trees and leafy hollows, well known to Peter and Janet, but I had never been far inside. To me it was still a place of curtained mystery, for the larch boughs swept low over the path, brushing us with their emerald tufts, and hazel catkins danced in the bushes powdering our noses with pollen as we passed. We did not seem to know exactly what we were aiming for, for we left the main track and made straight for the heart of the wood. There were pools of bluebells all round us, and the air was heavy with their cool scent.

"I never remember coming here before," said Janet, stopping suddenly and looking round her wonderingly. "In fact, I don't believe anyone ever comes here. Look, the trees are all bound together with honeysuckle tendrils, and there's no track through the bluebells—and oh, look! there's a place with the sun shining in, and there's kingcups on the ground! Come quick, Elaine! Let's go there."

I followed, blundering rather clumsily through the undergrowth, and when I got there, Janet was already standing in the middle of the clearing, still, awed, like some little sun-worshipper, and I stood very still too, looking about me. On each side of us were slender beeches, like pillars, their boughs meeting overhead in a feathery tracery of leaf and twig against the Spring sky. Between them young larches bowed their heads, and all up the centre was a swamp of bright kingcups, wide open, every flower brimful of sunshine. And on the beech boughs, like choristers singing in their stalls, the birds made melody. After the quiet of the deep woods it was almost deafening.

"Of course!" said Janet, turning to me with shining eyes, "it's Easter morning! And this is our Church! We'll walk up the kingcup aisle to the altar and see what happens."

The altar was the stump of a chestnut tree, but an off-shoot had sprung up behind it and was holding up candle-flowers to God. And just a little to the left was a wild cherry tree in full blossom, its snowy drifts scattering petals on the moss.

"It's a real, real Church," whispered Janet, sitting down by the altar, "there's the choir and the candles, the cherry tree preaching the sermon because it's so white. Let's read here, Elaine, let's read that bit Daddy read once about white robes. It was somewhere in Revelation."

We searched eagerly, and Janet found it fairly quickly and read the verses triumphantly. I did not know what they meant, but I loved the sound of them: "Thou hast a few names, even in Sardis, which have not defiled their garments; and they shall walk with me in white: for they are worthy. He that overcometh, the same shall be clothed in white raiment . . ."

"But what does it mean?" I urged. "What's Sardis?"

"It was a very wicked city," said Janet, knitting her brows, "and everyone was horrid and dirty except for just a very few people, and Jesus said those people should walk with Him . . . I suppose you do have to be very clean and white to walk with Jesus."

"How do you mean, horrid and dirty?" I asked. "What did they do?"

Janet stared at the dazzling purity of the cherry and didn't answer for a few minutes.

"I was just thinking," she said slowly at last, "that it must have been like it is at school sometimes—you know, Elaine, when they get together in the playground and whisper and giggle and talk about horrid things, and sometimes I go too and listen so as not to be different, and, you know, Mummy would have a fit if she heard some of the things Eileen and Gwynnedd talk about; and they say they see them at the cinema, but I believe they make half of it up—and Pete says the boys are worse than the girls."

I sat staring rather shamefacedly at the king-cups, for I had often been eager enough to listen myself, although I usually got pushed out.

"I think keeping your garments clean means refusing to listen and going away when they start," said Janet firmly. "I did it once, and they laughed and said I was a pious prig, and after that I was afraid. But from now onwards, Elaine, let's show them that we don't like it, because actually I believe quite a lot of the girls don't, and if we started, they might copy us, and in any case we'd have each other. Let's write down that text for to-day: 'They shall walk with Me in white, for they are worthy'."

We copied the verse carefully into our little notebooks, our heads bent low and the warm sunshine filtering through the foliage on to our hair. Then we rose to go, rather sadly, for perhaps we both knew that however often we might come back to our little Chapel, we should never recover the spell of that golden Easter morning, nor hear the birds singing again as they were singing then; the clear trills of blackbirds and thrushes mingled with the broken cooing of ring doves, and somewhere the call of the willowwren coming down the scale in semitones—and then, suddenly, the mocking cry of a cuckoo.

"First I've heard," said Janet, jerking us back from our dreams, "and she's early too. Come on, we'd better run, I ought to be helping Mummy."

She sped away, fleet of foot, through the woods and vaulted the gate out into the open meadows, and I followed, not far behind, for I was a much better runner than I used to be. The sun was quite high, and in the lamb meadows all the daisies and buttercups had opened their faces to the sun. Just at that moment it seemed almost impossible that there could be anything ugly and unclean and impure in such a bright world.

We got home to find the family in the midst of the usual Sunday commotion of getting into their best Sunday clothes. Frances had burst three buttons on her clean frock and was arguing loudly that she was too fat to wear it ever again. Johnny, who was mechanical, had just appeared with some pliers and a length of wire from his own private tool cupboard and was offering to lace her up down the back, "guaranteed not to bust." Blodwen, struggling with Lucy's socks, went into peals of good-natured laughter and remarked that you didn't need to go to the pictures for a bit of amusement, not if you lived in this family.

Robin was coming to Church too, as a treat, because it was Easter Sunday, and he was under the table very quietly dressing Jumbo up in Church clothes. In the general confusion of setting off and making certain that Cadwaller didn't set off too, Robin felt he had a fair chance of smuggling Jumbo into the service. In any case, there was no harm in trying.

Breakfast was great fun, as the Easter Rabbit had hidden coloured hard-boiled eggs all over the garden—one down under the daffodil trumpets, another deep in a clump of forget-me-nots, and a third in a deserted thrush's nest in the hawthorn hedge. They took a long time to find, and when we came in, our Sunday shoes were wet with dew and our Sunday hair wind-swept and unruly. The Easter Rabbit in the meantime was said to be reading over his sermon in his study.

Breakfast over, we all got ready to the usual motherly cry of, "Have you all got your collection, and have you all remembered your handkerchiefs?" A final struggle with Cadwaller and we were all off, prancing across the meadows and tossing our hats in the air, because Mrs. Owen was staying at home with Lucy, and Blodwen had no idea of keeping us in order.

The church was overflowing with people and

full of Easter flowers. The Communion Table was a mass of huge daffodil trumpets, white blossom, and tulips, and the choir and congregation rose to their feet and sang as only the Welsh can sing:

>*"Jesus Christ is risen to-day,*
> *Alleluia!"*

I glanced along our pew. Blodwen's head was thrown far back, and she was almost bursting through her new purple blouse on the high notes at the end of the verses. She had not noticed Jumbo arrayed in a flowery handkerchief and a pair of trousers beating time with his trunk. Then Mr. Owen read the story of the Resurrection and how the Angel of the Lord came down and opened the tomb in raiment white as snow, and I thought of the Lord Jesus coming forth, no doubt in shining robes to match the Angel. To walk close to Him in the path of life, sharing His fulness of joy, one would need to be very clean and pure too. Janet was right; nothing dirty or soiling could stay near that radiance.

We rose again to sing the second hymn. Peter in the choir had a solo part in this one, and his voice, clear and unbroken, seemed to soar right to the roof:

"Jesus lives! For us He died!
Then, alone to Jesus living,
Pure in heart may we abide,
Glory to our Saviour giving.
Alleluia!"

But at that moment Mr. Owen glanced at Robin, and a queer look came over his face. And Robin, noticed at last, scrambled up on the seat behind Blodwen and, holding Jumbo high above the heads of the congregation, he waggled its little grey trunk joyfully at his father.

CHAPTER XII

"WHEN THE GARDEN
CAME ALIVE"

NEXT MORNING there were two great items of news that put everything else out of our heads: Philippa was coming home again, and Peter's rabbits had babies.

The morning post arrived during breakfast, and there was a letter from Mrs. Thomas, Philippa's mother, announcing their intended arrival on Wednesday and asking Mrs. Owen to get in a woman from the village to see that the house was ready. And this caused a great deal of talk and excitement among the children, for Philippa was a friend of theirs and had done everything with them before her illness.

I knew all about Philippa too. She lived in the house belonging to my garden and had caught polio just a year ago. She had been very ill indeed, but although she got much better in the end, her legs had remained partly paralysed. Her father was in the Navy and was usually away, and Philippa had been at a special hospital learning to walk again, while her mother stayed in rooms nearby.

"Can Philippa walk again?" asked Janet eagerly.

"Only a very little, with crutches," answered Mrs. Owen, sadly, "but of course she may still go on getting better. Poor Philippa! We must do all we can to give her a big welcome, and show her that we still want to play with her."

Every face at the table lighted up with eager interest, except mine, for I was feeling very uncomfortable. Johnnie and Francie planned to fill the room with flowers, and Janet said she was going to make some sweets. Peter, who was quite good at carpentering, wanted to make her a little bedside table if his father would find him the wood. Mr. Owen thought this a very good idea, and they went off together to see what could be done about it.

Robin said nothing, but he sat thinking deeply and went rather red in the face. When the room was empty and the children had scattered, he tugged at his mother's apron and looked up at her, his blue eyes brimming with tears.

"Dat little girl," he whispered, "what hasn't got no legs—I'll lend her Jumbo."

"Will you, darling?" said Mrs. Owen, stooping down to him and understanding the greatness of his sacrifice. "Then we'll take him up together and put him on Philippa's bed just before she arrives, and she'll be so, so pleased."

"Not to stay," whispered Robin, nervously, "just . . . just till I go to bed."

"Yes, just till you go to bed," agreed Mrs. Owen. "I think Jumbo might feel homesick if he spent the night away from you . . . Whatever's the matter, Peter? What's happened?"

There was a sort of stampede on the stairs, and Peter hurled himself into the room, breathless with excitement, with Janet behind him.

"My rabbits, Mummy!" he cried. "They've had babies! She's pulled all the fur off her tummy and made a nest in the closed half of the hutch. Do come and see—no, not you, Elaine and Robin— one at a time—the father eats them if too many people look at them."

"You'll have to take the father away and put him by himself, Peter," said Mr. Owen, coming in. "They often kill their babies if you leave them in the hutch. Just let Mummy and Elaine have a peep, and then give the mother a good feed of bran and dandelions, and leave her alone."

I seized Mrs. Owen's hand and tiptoed to the

hutch, Robin hiding behind us. Very carefully Peter opened the door, just a chink, and we saw a mass of soft white fur, as though someone had been blowing hundreds of dandelion clocks. In the middle was a pink mass of squirming, squeaking baby rabbits.

"How many?" I whispered.

"Dunno!" answered Peter softly. "They all seem stuck together, and I don't like to touch them to count. We'll leave them alone for a day or two till she gets used to them. Daddy, instead of a bedside table, could I make a new rabbit hutch? Then Philippa could have two baby rabbits; she could have them by the bed, and they'd be good company."

"I don't know what Mrs. Thomas would think about the smell," answered Mr. Owen, "but she could have them just outside the window in any case; I expect they'll make her a bedroom on the ground floor. That's a very good idea, Pete. You carry on!"

Mr. Owen went back to his study, and I ran after him and poked my worried little face round the door. To my surprise and relief he seemed to have guessed my thoughts.

"Come in, Elaine," he said, and I went and leaned up against his shoulder. "You're thinking about that shell, aren't you, and wondering where it's got to? I took it out of the Museum that same night, and it's here safe in my desk. Would you like to go with Mummy when she goes up this morning to get ready, and slip it back into its proper place? And one other thing I thought of: you started to make a pretty good job of the garden, and you've got two days left in which to work hard. How about finishing off that little rockery you started and tidying it up a bit?"

I was thrilled; somehow, since the day of my great discovery I had not wanted to go back to the garden. It had seemed a guilty, fearful place, and yet I had missed it and had wondered what my seeds were doing and whether the eggs had hatched. No I could return, not hiding any longer. Of course, it was only for two days, but it was better than nothing.

I was all ready to start when Mrs. Owen appeared, to go up and open the door for the woman who was to clean. In one hand I clasped the shell, in the other I carried a trowel, and Mrs. Owen asked no questions when I slipped in at the front door and over to the cabinet. I did not look at the garden till I had done this, but when the shell was safely back in its place, I ran out into my little kingdom and explored it from end to end.

It was amazing what the April sun and rain had done. The little plants on my rockery were choked with skutch and dandelion, but underneath them I could see opening buds. Tulips held up flaming cups, and forget-me-nots massed the borders, and as I wandered round I smelt a sweet fragrance and searched in the tall weeds until I found clusters of lily of the valley longing for the light. Last of all, I tiptoed to the lilac bush, already in bud, and peeped at my nest. There was a rustling and a cheeping, and five yellow beaks were opened wide. I laughed softly, and drew down the leafy curtain.

"They thought I was their mother, bringing a worm," I whispered to myself, "I wonder where she's gone?"

She kept darting past as I knelt at my weeding, and both she and I worked hard all that day and the next. I cleared the rockery completely and set free gay little patches of Virginia stock, Iceland poppies, and cushions of pink arabis and forget-me-nots. I made a space round the lilies of the valley and the tulips, and Mrs. Owen and the children were quite surprised at what I'd done. I could hardly tear myself away for meals and worked on till the last light faded, breathing in the scent of newly turned earth and wallflowers, and sometimes running across to kneel in front of the white bells to catch a breath of their fragrance. I was happy and sad both at once—happy because I was setting free the garden, sad because it was mine no longer. In such a little while it would all belong to Philippa.

On the last morning everyone came up with Mrs. Owen to arrange and inspect and bring their gifts. Peter had worked as hard as I had, and the hutch, very bright and green and sticky, was set proudly in the middle of the lawn at the side of the house to wait until the baby rabbits came of age. Janet arranged plates of home-made fudge in every nook and cranny, and the house was decked with spring flowers. Philippa's couch was drawn up to the window, all complete with Jumbo, overlooking the rockery. Everything was ready, except for the garden. I still hadn't weeded round the roots of the lilac tree.

"Well," said Mrs. Owen, looking round, "I think we'd better go home to dinner. Someone's bringing them by car about four o'clock, so we'll come up then and have tea ready."

I tugged at her sleeve. "Please," I whispered, "need I come to dinner? Can I stay and finish the weeding?"

I whispered because I was so afraid Peter and

Janet might offer to stay and help too, and on this last afternoon I wanted to be alone with my garden. But they had already hurried hungrily ahead, and only Mrs. Owen and I remained.

"All right," she answered smilingly, "I'll send you up a little picnic in a red-spotted handkerchief. Johnny can bring it."

I breathed a sigh of relief. Johnny was very fond of his food and would certainly not wish to stay. Mrs. Owen shut the gate behind her, and just for a couple of hours I could be alone.

Johnny cane and went in a great hurry, but I was too busy to bother about food just then. I was cleaning the roots of the lilac, when I suddenly heard the squeak of motor brakes outside, the opening of doors and the sound of voices. Then I heard the latch click and realised what had happened. They had come earlier than expected.

I dived round the corner of the house like a frightened rabbit and pressed myself against the wall. I was unreasonably terrified of being caught red-handed and alone in the garden, and only hoped I could escape without being seen. But I was only just in time, for the next moment I heard the delighted voice of a child cry out.

"Oh, Mummy, Mummy, the garden's alive, and we thought it would be all choked! And oh, look,

Mummy, the lilies of the valley are out—and oh, LOOK, Mummy, someone's made a little rockery!"

"Why," replied a woman's voice, "it's just as though fairies had been at work; how beautiful it looks. And, look, there are . . ."

But she was interrupted by a scream from the child. "Oh, Mummy, Mummy, there's a rabbit hutch on the lawn round the side of the house. Come, quick, and see if there's a rabbit inside!"

I knew I was lost, and stood there looking as guilty as though I had committed a robbery, and the next moment Philippa's head came round the wall.

She was small and thin, leaning on crutches, her legs supported by irons. But I thought she was beautiful, for her fair plaits hung below her waist, and her eyes were like wide-open forget-me-nots. They seemed to fill up most of her pale little face, and she stood staring at me in frightened astonishment.

"Mummy," she called sharply, "come quick! There's someone hiding behind the wall!"

Mrs. Thomas, her head full of burglars, came rushing round the corner with a little cry of alarm. But when she saw how small I was, she stopped short.

"What are you doing here, little girl?" she asked sternly.

"Nothing," I stammered guiltily, "at least . . . I was gardening. Mrs. Owen said I could . . . I live with the Owens. We all came to get ready for Philippa."

Mrs. Thomas burst out laughing.

"Why," she said, "you must be Elaine, who saw our burglar! Mrs. Owen wrote and told us all about it. So it's you who have worked in our garden! Well, Philippa and I think that it's all simply beautiful, and you must come and welcome us inside the house. Come along, Phil, you've been standing long enough."

She took a key from her pocket and picked up Philippa as lightly as though she'd been a baby, and carried her into the house. She laid her on the couch where Jumbo lay awaiting her in flowery pants and a bonnet.

"Oh, Mummy, the flowers!" cried Philippa. "Look at the rockery, just underneath the window where I can see it all day. Do you know, Elaine, all the time I've been in hospital I've lain in bed and looked at a brick wall and a laundry chimney. There just aren't any flowers in Manchester. Now sit down and tell me who made the fudge, and who put this funny elephant here. And oh, was there a rabbit in that hutch?"

My tongue was unloosed, and I poured out all the news, while Mrs. Thomas bustled round the kitchen. At one point she poked her head round the door.

"Have you had dinner, Elaine?" she asked.

I suddenly rememberd my picnic and dashed off to fetch it. I sat and ate my sandwiches, while Philippa ate an omelette, and then we all had a cup of tea and sugar biscuits. Then Mrs. Thomas got up firmly.

"If the family is coming to welcome us this afternoon," she said, "Philippa must have a rest. Elaine, we'll see you again later, and we are just thrilled with the garden."

So I said goodbye to Philippa and skipped all the way home in the sunshine. The garden was mine no longer, but I felt happier about it than I'd ever felt before.

"It's a funny thing," I thought, "but it's much more fun doing things for other people than just doing them for myself." And I leaped over a hummock for joy, as I thought of Philippa lying on the couch, her small white face turned to the rockery.

CHAPTER XIII

"YE DID IT NOT TO ME"

THE EASTER HOLIDAYS raced by, and I found myself busier and happier than I had ever been before. For one thing I was getting much stronger and tougher and could climb easy trees and puff along behind the others in their chases. And instead of thinking their games were silly, I was beginning to enjoy them. Besides, the beauty of the spring countryside was taking hold of me too, and I'd become intensely interested in nests and wild flowers. Janet was never tired of teaching me their names, and Peter loved showing off his knowledge, so I was on the way to becoming quite a naturalist.

Then there was Philippa. The children all did their best to cheer her up, but, strange to say, she took a fancy to me and seemed to prefer my company to that of anyone else. Perhaps it was because we were both only children, and both had lonely little fancies and secrets that brothers and sisters in a large family could never understand; or perhaps it was that I was less energetic than the others and found it easier to sit still. In any case, I was pleased to be, for the first time in my life, the favourite, and to begin with I visited Philippa every day. I went on working in the garden, too, and Mrs. Thomas gave me a patch all to myself in which to grow flowers. This was a great joy to me, and I used to potter about in it with Philippa lying on a rug on the grass nearby. But when the earth was ready and the seeds were planted, there was no more to do but wait, and the following day we all went out for a picnic; and the day after that the three of us cycled along the coast to look for gulls' eggs. So that what with one thing and another it was only on the evening of the third day that I went back to Philippa.

She was lying by her open window, and I hopped nimbly in over the sill and sat down on her couch. But she did not seem at all pleased to see me, and at first wouldn't answer me when I spoke to her.

"Whatever's the matter?" I asked rather crossly. "If you won't speak to me, I'll go away."

She turned her face toward me, her big blue eyes full of tears.

"Why didn't you come?" she whispered. "I've

waited two whole days all by myself, and you just forgot about me. You don't care about me a bit."

"I do!" I answered rather impatiently. "I didn't forget about you at all. We were just busy. I'm sorry, honestly I am, Phil, but we went to the Caves, and down to the sea, and Peter and Janet wanted me to go with them, and . . ."

I stopped, for she had buried her white little face in the pillow and was sobbing bitterly.

"And I can't ever do anything again," she gasped, "I expect I shall always be a cripple, and no one will ever go on being my friend! Oh, I wish I could die!"

I was feeling really sorry for her now, and I flung my arm round her shoulders.

"I *will* go on being your friend, Phil," I said in real distress. "Only I must go with the others sometimes. I'm awfully sorry you're a cripple, and I'll come whenever I can. But you mustn't be cross if I don't some days, because soon it will be school, and I shall be rather busy with prep. and things. But I promise I'll do my best."

"Don't you like coming to see me?" asked Philippa, turning over and sniffing pathetically.

" 'Course I do," I answered, "but I like doing things with Jan too sometimes." I was beginning to think that Philippa was rather selfish.

"Oh, I know you like Jan far better than me," replied Philippa, and disappeared again under the bedclothes. And because I had never been ill myself, and because no one had brought me up to care much about other people, I soon got impatient and went off home, saying as a parting shot that I'd come back when she was in a better temper.

The Summer term started soon after that, and I was busier than ever. I had ceased to enjoy Philippa's company very much, because she usually spent most of the time grumbling and sulking because I hadn't been the day before, and we often quarrelled. I had quite forgotten that I, too, had once felt left out and sorry for myself with far less reason than Philippa. And not being used to making myself do things that I didn't like, my visits became fewer and fewer. Janet did her best, but she got rather tired of always being questioned as to where I was and why I hadn't come.

"You'd better go to-day," said Janet rather anxiously one afternoon as we cycled home from school. "She likes you much better than me now."

"I don't see why I should," I answered crossly. "She's so spoiled and selfish. All she does is to grumble and ask why I don't come every day. She can't expect me to do nothing but sit with her."

Janet was silent. Then she sighed. "It must be pretty awful," she said thoughtfully, "never being able to run about. I sometimes think, Elaine . . . I wish we could tell her about Jesus. She'd be much happier then. Daddy's talked lots to Mrs. Thomas, but she never comes to Church, and Philippa never says her prayers or reads the Bible. Mrs. Thomas once said that if there was really a God, why did Philippa become a cripple?—and she couldn't be bothered with religion. I heard Daddy telling Mummy, but don't say, because I wasn't meant to be listening."

I felt rather uncomfortable, because I had thought the same thing. But I knew it was no good trying to tell Philippa about Jesus if I quarrelled with her and got impatient and didn't bother to go and see her. I remembered Janet's words the night on which I had become a Christian: "Daddy said it wouldn't have been much good telling you . . . because we were so selfish."

Well, I would have to think it all out, but not just then, because we were just reaching home, and I was hungry. I bounced into the kitchen, where tea was laid, and ate five thick slices of bread and jam and drank four cups of tea. Mrs. Owen laughed at me.

"Elaine," she said as I rose to go, "we'll have to

weigh you. You've put on pounds in the Easter holidays, and I don't believe your mother would know you. The country agrees with you. I think you'll have to stay with us for ever."

I grinned at her and danced out of the door— under the snowy may trees throwing long evening shadows across the fields, up the hill where the daisies and buttercups were beginning to close their petals. I danced all the way, for I had never felt quite so strong and alive and skippety before. Yes, Mrs. Owen was right; the country suited me, and I never, never wanted to go back to London again. I should like to see Mummy again occasionally, but she must come and vist me here— here in this land of light and song and colour that was the month of May.

I arrived all rosy and breathless at Philippa's window and came down to earth with a bump at the sight of her pale, cross little face. A delicious tea with a plate of iced cakes lay untasted beside her. I sat with my back to them because they made my mouth water so.

"Why didn't you come yesterday?" began Philippa as usual. "I waited for you all the evening."

"Too much prep.," I answered shortly, "and I can't stay long to-night. We only got in from school at half-past four; we were late coming up from games. Do you know, Philippa, we've started playing tennis, it's super fun!"

"I wish I could play tennis," sighed Philippa, "or even go to school! It's awfully dull always doing lessons alone. I've been trying to-day, but it's no fun. Tell me what lessons you do, Elaine. I wonder if they are the same as mine."

For once she seemed willing to listen to me instead of talking about her own troubles, so I chattered on gaily for a time. We were getting on much better than usual, and I wondered if I could possibly tell her about the Bible and the Lord Jesus.

"What lesson do you like best?" she asked, when I'd stopped talking and had sat silent for a minute wondering how to begin.

"Well," I answered rather hesitantly, "I quite like all lessons, but what I like best isn't a school lesson at all. It's a sort of lesson Jan and I do together before breakfast. We read the Bible together and choose a text for the day and write it down, and it sort of helps us all day. Do you ever read the Bible, Phil?"

She shook her head, but looked at me rather curiously. "Mrs. Owen once talked to me about it and gave me a book of Bible stories," she said, "but

Mummy says the real Bible isn't suitable for children, and I used to think it awfully dull when we read it at school prayers. Do you really like it, Elaine?"

I nodded. "I used to be like you," I said, "and my mummy never told me anything about it. I thought it was just a big black dull book full of long words, until I came to the Owens. But then, one day, something happened to me."

"What?" asked Philippa, her blue eyes very big and solemn.

"Well," I answered slowly, not quite knowing how to explain, "I did something rather naughty, and I was all miserable and frightened, and I ran away into a wood. And Mr. Owen came to look for me, and we stayed in the wood ages, and he told me that if I told Jesus about the wrong things I'd done He'd forgive me and make them white, and after that I'd always belong to Him."

"And what happened then?" asked Philippa.

"Well," I answered slowly, "I did it, and now I do belong to Him."

"And what difference does it make?" asked Philippa. There seemed to be an almost mocking look in those great blue eyes that I could not quite understand.

"Well," I said hesitatingly, "I've been ever so

much happier since. You see, if you belong to Jesus, it's like having a Friend you can tell things to. I don't get all frightened and miserable like I used to. You sort of feel safe. He tells you what to do in the Bible every day, and if you do it, it's like staying close beside Him, and then you are always happy."

"And what else?" went on Philippa. "Is that all?"

"Well, it's quite a lot," I answered rather crossly, "but of course there are other things as well. Jesus teaches you to be good."

"And are you good?" demanded Philippa.

"I'm better than I used to be," I replied, fidgeting rather uncomfortably. "I never get cross now like I used to. I was always getting angry and losing my temper and being horrid, and now I don't —at least, not very often."

"Oh!" said Philippa, in a voice I didn't like at all. There was an uncomfortable pause. I glanced at the clock.

"I must fly!" I cried, jumping to my feet. "I'll never finish my prep. Shall I bring you my Bible next time, Phil? And then you can see for yourself."

"All right," said Philippa rather coldly. "You can bring it if you like. I want you to come to tea the day after to-morrow, Saturday. Will you come, Elaine, for certain sure?"

I was halfway through the door in a hurry to be off. "O.K.," I answered, my mind on my belated prep. "I expect I can come. I'll do my best."

"No, no," shouted Philippa, "you've got to promise. It's very special this time. You will come, won't you?"

"Yes, all right," I called back rather impatiently, because Philippa often said things were special when I couldn't see anything special about them. "I said I'd come, so don't worry."

But as I ran down the hill, Philippa's words rang in my ears, although I did not want to think about them. "What difference does it make? Are you good?"

I was certainly happier, but was I really nicer? Or was it just that Peter and Janet were so much nicer to me? What was I like with selfish, spoiled people? What was I like with weak, ill people? Was I really patient and kind? And why had Philippa looked at me like that?

My prep. forgotten I wandered slowly home, idly pulling the heads off the cow parsley and chewing grass. It was after sunset when I reached the gate—everything looked gentle and blue and shadowed.

"Jan," I said that night, when we sat curled up up on my bed in our nightgowns, talking, "do you remember that bit your father showed you in the Bible, that night I ran away? Something about hungry people and ill people?"

"Yes," said Janet, "I underlined it in red, and it was in Matthew. I was going to show it you, but I forgot. Here it is—Matthew 25."

She read it slowly and reverently, and I listened to it all, but certain words stayed specially in my mind: "I was sick . . . and ye visited Me not . . . Inasmuch as ye did it not to one of the least of these, ye did it not to Me."

CHAPTER XIV

A BIRTHDAY REMEMBERED

SATURDAY WAS ANOTHER beautiful day, and as we gathered round the dinner table, Janet suddenly looked out of the open window and said, "Mummy, couldn't we take tea to the river and bathe this afternoon?"

A joyful uproar greeted this suggestion, for we had not bathed that year. Mrs. Owen glanced a little doubtfully out of doors, but the still golden sunshine reassured her, and she said, when she could make herself heard, that she thought it would be a very good idea.

"Come with us, Daddy," coaxed Johnny, climbing on to his father's knee, "you said you'd teach me to swim."

The children flung themselves on him in a body at this suggestion, for he was a very busy man and his company was a rare treat. But he shook his head sadly.

"Got to get into my best black suit and marry

someone," he said with a sigh. He gazed out at the daisied slopes and the sparkling blue sea in the distance. "Fancy wanting to get married on an afternoon like this when you could be splashing in the river!"

"Never mind, Daddy," comforted Peter, "you'll get a super tea."

"Maybe," said his father, "but I'd rather eat buns in the mud with you. Never mind! I'll keep next Saturday free and take you all to the beach—mothers, babies, prams, dogs, and all! Don't ask me how! We'd better borrow the parish hearse."

He scattered the children and went off to get ready, and we rushed in all directions collecting fishing rods, sandwiches, lemonade, Cadwaller, and towels. Then we stood round expectantly, as Mrs. Owen brought out the bathing things from a suitcase where they'd been all the winter in newspaper and mothballs. Our joy was a little clouded by Robin, who had just discovered that he was not to be one of the party and was standing in the middle of the room, crimson in the face, roaring like a bull. But his legs were too small and fat to keep up, and besides, Mrs. Owen was afraid of his getting drowned. She was even a little nervous about Frances. "Don't you think, Francie . . ." she began doubtfully.

"No, Mummy, I really don't," interrupted Frances, going stiff with agitation. And Peter and Janet and I all came in heavily on her side and pleaded for her till Mrs. Owen gave in.

"We'll look after her ever so well," promised Peter, "and anyhow, the river's so shallow, we couldn't drown her if we wanted to."

"Which we don't," added Johnny.

"No, I know," answered Mrs. Owen, "but remember she's only small, and dry her properly, Janet, and don't sit around in wet bathing things, and Elaine, don't stay in too long, and don't forget . . ."

"No, Mummy—Yes, Mummy—we won't forget anything, we promise," we shouted, all kissing her goodbye at once and dashing off up the hill, leaving her standing on the doorstep calling out last-minute instructions, which were completely drowned by Robin's roars.

We climbed the hill beneath great shady trees that had twisted their old gnarled roots across the path, making it impossible for prams and bicycles. Out on the uplands the view stretched away in front of us, bathed in sunshine—rolling hills and deep valleys dotted with white Welsh farms in the midst of emerald sheep pastures. The higher slopes were clothed in new bracken now, and the beeches

were transparent with light. Never had I seen such
greenness, and the little wind that ruffled our hair
was fragrant with the scent of hawthorn. We all
went mad and pushed each other about and
laughed till we couldn't stop over nothing at all, as
happy children will when the spring has got into
their blood.

We had reached the top of the valley where the
path dipped steeply down to the river. Already we
could see the golden-brown water flecked with
sunshine filtering through the boughs of the willow
trees, when I suddenly remembered. I stood stock
still, staring at that beckoning little path twisting
down through banks of late bluebell, campion,
and cow parsley. I could hear the river laughing
and chattering over the stones.

"Whatever's the matter?" asked Janet, turning
round to see why I'd stopped. "Have you swallowed a fly?"

"I've just remembered," I answered slowly, "I
promised . . . I said I'd go to tea with Philippa."

There was a long, dismayed silence. Then Janet
spoke.

"You'd better go back, I suppose," she said
flatly. "Or . . . if you like very much . . . I suppose
I could go back instead. I mean, if it was a promise, I suppose someone had better keep it."

"Come on, you girls," shouted Peter. He had reached the bank and had already changed into his bathing trunks. Johnny and Frances were struggling with their buttons, knee-deep in cuckoo flowers.

I stood thinking deeply. Yes, I said I'd go back and take my Bible. If I failed, she'd never believe that the Bible made any difference to anyone. I stared again at that inviting little path, and it reminded me of my special verse: "Thou wilt show me the path of life . . . in Thy Presence is fulness of joy." And suddenly I knew very clearly what path He was showing me that afternoon, not the path that led down to the cool, dancing river, but the one that led back over the uplands to Philippa, the path of self-denial and kindness and keeping one's promises. That was where I should find Him. "I was sick, and ye visited me," and "In Thy Presence is fulness of joy."

I drew a long breath and turned back.

"I'd better go," I said shortly. "Goodbye, have a nice time."

"Goodbye," answered Janet, much relieved. "We'll come again another time—there'll be lots more chances to bathe," and she rushed off down the valley unfastening her dress as she ran.

It seemed a long, hot walk home, and I tried

hard not to think of the others splashing in the golden water. Yet I was not really as unhappy as I thought I would be. I think it was the first time in my life I had given up doing something I minded about for the sake of someone else, and it was a strange, rather pleasant feeling. I reached the house at last and fetched my Bible unnoticed, for Mrs. Owen had taken the two babies out for a walk, and Blodwen was busy in the kitchen. When I reached Philippa's house, it was after half-past four, and Mrs. Thomas was standing at the gate looking rather anxious.

"Oh, Elaine," she said in a relieved voice, "I'm so glad you've come. You see, it's Philippa's birthday, and I was going to have a party, but she wanted you all by yourself, and she said you'd promised to come. She was getting in such a state, thinking you'd forgotten."

She led me into the garden where Philippa lay in a deck chair by the rockery with tea spread out beside her, and a beautiful pink birthday cake with ten candles. She looked very pretty in a new blue summer frock she had as a present, and I hot and rumpled, in my oldest clothes and muddiest shoes, felt rather ashamed of myself.

"Where have you been?" asked Philippa. "I

thought you'd forgotten. You didn't know it was my birthday, did you?"

"No," I answered, "or I'd have brought you a present. Many happy returns of the day, Philippa. I'm sorry I'm late, but the others went bathing in the river, and I went some of the way with them, and then came back by myself."

"Oh," said Philippa, with that curious look in her eyes that seemed to size me up, "and why did you do that? Did you forget you were coming to tea with me?"

"Well, yes," I replied truthfully, "I did just at first, because Pete only thought of bathing at dinner, suddenly, and we all got rather excited. But as soon as I remembered, I came back quick."

"Oh, I see," said Philippa in her queer pointed way. Then she added, "Do you like bathing?"

"Mm, ever so," I answered. "But it doesn't matter. Mr. Owen's going to take us to the sea next week. We're not allowed to bathe alone in the sea, but the river's shallow. Even Francie went."

Our conversation was cut short by Mrs. Thomas arriving with the teapot, and we had a very happy tea party. The garden was a riot of flowers now, and the first bees were humming in the lavender bushes. Mrs. Thomas told us funny stories, and I stuffed myself with cakes and biscuits and sandwiches. Then we lit the candles, which didn't show at all in the sunshine, and Philippa cut the cake.

When even I could eat no more, Mrs. Thomas rose and picked up the tray.

"I'm going to wash up the tea things now," she said, "and leave you two together. Philippa, do you want to show Elaine your presents?"

"Later," said Philippa, "but we'll stay here for a bit now, because we've got a secret." She waited till her mother had disappeared, and then she turned to me eagerly. "Have you brought your Bible, Elaine?" she asked.

"Yes," I answered, rather surprised, for she had not seemed particularly interested before, "it's here under my chair. I'll show it you."

"It's like this," said Philippa. "I've been thinking. You said that when you know Jesus, it makes you good, and I think I'll believe you now, because you came back from bathing when I know you wanted to go. If you hadn't come back, I'd have thought it was all silly pretending. And you said it was like having a Friend you could tell things to, and I just wondered—if I read my Bible and prayed, do you think Jesus would make me walk again?"

I hesitated. "He *could* make you walk again,"

I said simply. "He did it lots of times. He was always making people better. Jan and I are reading Mark in the morning, and it's all stories about people who were ill and got healed."

"Well, read me one," commanded Philippa.

"I'll read what I read this morning," I said confidently. "It was about a man who couldn't walk at all, so they let him down through the roof, and first of all Jesus said, 'Your sins be forgiven', and then He made him walk—here it is, I've found it," and I read her the story of the paralysed man in Mark 2, and she listened intently, her eyes fixed on my face.

"It said in the notes," I remarked thoughtfully, "that the most important thing is to have your sins forgiven—then you can start asking for other things."

Philippa frowned. "I don't think I've got an awful lot of sins," she said. "How could I, lying here? I couldn't really be very naughty if I tried."

"You can be cross," I answered candidly, "and you grumble rather. I think that counts as sin. I used to be terribly cross before I loved Jesus."

"You still are, sometimes," retorted Philippa, "but never mind, don't let's quarrel to-day. Tell me how you get your sins forgiven."

"You just ask," I said simply, "and you believe that Jesus died for you . . . that's all, I think."

Philippa shook her head. "I don't believe it's as easy as all that," she said firmly. "Don't lets bother about sins. Let's just ask Jesus to make me walk. Do you know how, Elaine?"

I looked doubtful. "I don't think you can do it like that, Philippa," I answered, feeling quite out of my depth. "I'm sure you've got to belong to Jesus first. Let me ask Mrs. Owen about it, and then I'll come and tell you."

"All right," said Philippa, "you ask her. I don't believe you know an awful lot about it yourself, Elaine. Now come and see my presents."

I helped her indoors and admired her beautiful gifts, and then I said Goodbye and Thank You to Mrs. Thomas, and went trotting home. To my surprise the others had not returned. Lucy was in bed, and Robin in the sand pile. It was one of those very rare occasions on which I could have Mrs. Owen all to myself. She was in the kitchen ironing Sunday clothes.

"Auntie," I said, sitting myself on the table and swinging my legs, "I want to ask you something very important. Can you pray for things before you've had your sins forgiven?"

She looked up startled. "Have you come home, Elaine?" she asked. "Where are the others?"

"I forgot I promised to go to tea with Philippa," I explained shortly, "so I came back . . . and Philippa wants to know. She wants me to pray that she'll get better, but she doesn't want to bother about having her sins forgiven. She says she hasn't got many."

Mrs. Owen switched off her iron and gave the subject her whole attention. I discovered later that she prayed each day for Philippa and her mother.

"It tells us in the Bible that God is so pure and holy that we can't come to Him at all until we've been made clean and been forgiven by the Lord Jesus," she answered. "But of course no one can really pray for forgiveness until they see how much they need it. I think . . ."

But I never heard what Mrs. Owen thought, for to my extreme annoyance the back door was flung open at that moment and the children burst into the kitchen, sunburnt, untidy, and noisy, trailing wet bathing things and wild flowers, with Cadwaller covered in mud leaping behind them. Our peace was shattered.

"Mummy," announced Peter, "there were some boy scouts in tents by the river, camping. Mummy, please, can we all go camping?"

Mrs. Owen blinked, as she always did when switched too suddenly from one subject to another. "Why, yes, Peter," she answered, "I think it would be lovely. But you didn't mean to-night, did you?"

"No, Mummy, not to-night," said Peter, in the patient voice he used when explaining things to Robin. "We should need weeks and weeks to get ready. We should need stores and a compass, and a map, and two tents, and a ground sheet, and sleeping bags. I mean in the summer holidays. You said we couldn't afford all to go somewhere together, but camping wouldn't cost anything at all. We'd go to the mountains, and we'd go on bikes, and you and the babies and the gear could come on the bus. We'd go in Daddy's holiday, and he'd take us up Snowdon."

"Who's taking me up Snowdon?" said the Vicar, coming in at that moment and flinging himself down rather wearily in the old kitchen rocking chair, and holding out his arms to Frances, who leaped joyfully into his lap.

"Mummy says we can go camping in the mountains this Summer," said Peter eagerly. "You said you'd take us climbing this year, didn't you, Daddy?"

"Why, yes," agreed Mr. Owen, as eager as Peter. "I've been waiting for years for you to be old enough to start on the big mountains, and I'd have taken you all last August, only you spoiled it by having chickenpox. It will be extra good fun this year, because we shall have Elaine with us. We need to find a farmhouse for Mummy and the babies, and one tent for me and Pete and Johnny and one for the girls."

"Me in the tent," whispered Frances, "oh, say I can be in the tent!"

"Of course," answered Mr. Owen, "I'm not sleeping out in the wilds of Snowdonia without Francie to look after me!" And he drew her smooth mousy head against his shoulder, and they sat quietly enjoying each other. There were no favourites in the family, but I used to think that shy, dreamy little Frances had a corner in her father's heart that was shared by no one else.

CHAPTER XV

A SUDDEN MEETING

I WAS SO ANXIOUS to finish my conversation with Mrs. Owen that as soon as our lights were out that night I slipped out of bed and crept downstairs in my nightgown. Mr. Owen was getting ready his Sunday sermon in his study, and Mrs. Owen was sitting alone in the living-room darning socks. I sat down on the hearthrug, leaned my head against her knees and went on from where I'd left off.

"It's funny Philippa doesn't think she's got any sins," I began, "because she's really awfully selfish and cross. Couldn't you come and explain it to her, Auntie?"

She was silent for a moment, and then, instead of answering me, she said, "I'll tell you a story, and you try to think what it means."

I curled round, looking up into her face, and she started off, threading her needle in and out of a big darn as she talked.

"There was once an old woman who lived in a little village on the mountains, and one day in winter she went to town, and she bought a packet of Washo, which, as you know from the advertisements, WASHES CLOTHES WHITER. She washed her linen and hung it out on Monday, and it certainly did look whiter than the clothes in the other cottage gardens. She was so pleased that she left it out for two whole days, so that everyone could see it.

"But on Tuesday afternoon it was bitterly cold, and she thought, 'I must bring it in before nightfall'. So out she went, but when she got into the garden, she threw up her hands in horror and said, 'Who's been meddling with my washing? It's not really white any more—in fact, it looks almost grey'.

"No one had meddled with her washing, and in a moment or two she realised what had happened. While she was busy indoors, the snow had fallen on the mountains, and against that pure dazzling whiteness even her Washo washing seemed grey. She had seen God's whiteness, and that made all the difference."

She glanced at me, smiling, but I was frowning in a puzzled way, not quite understanding.

"Lots of people are like that old woman," said

Mrs. Owen. "They just look at their neighbours, and they say, 'I'm not a sinner', 'I'm better than So-and-so', and 'I don't steal like So-and-so', and 'I'm much less selfish than So-and-so'. And they quite forget that God never tells them to be like So-and-so. He says, 'Be ye holy, as I am holy', and He sent Jesus to show us just how perfect and holy He was. It's when we look at Jesus in the Bible that we see God's perfect shining whiteness, perfect courage, perfect goodness, perfect love. And the more we look, the more we cry out, 'I am not like that'. It's like the story of Peter in the 5th of Luke. He thought he was a very nice man till Jesus came into his boat, but then he cried, 'Depart from me, for I am a sinful man, O Lord!' "

"I see," I answered slowly, "I've got to keep telling Philippa about Jesus, and when she sees what He's like, she'll see what she's like, and till then, I suppose she mustn't ask to be made better."

Mrs. Owen shook her head, smiling.

"Lots of people came to Jesus in the Bible who only thought about getting better," she said simply. "I expect the leper was just thinking about his sores, and I don't suppose little children knew why they came at all, but Jesus rebuked the disciples who tried to send them away. He was so kind and merciful that He always said, 'Come'.

He never turned anyone away. He just gave them more than they asked for. He let them see His face and hear His voice, and I expect that was far more wonderful to them than being healed. You let Philippa pray any way she likes; the Lord Jesus Himself will teach her as she comes to Him in prayer and will show her her need of forgiveness and lead her to God. You've got just three things to do."

"What?" I asked.

"First, pray for her, and we all will too. Then, secondly, make special times to go and read the Bible with her, and stick to them faithfully. Lastly, show her the love and care and patience of the Lord Jesus in your own life. If He is really living in your heart, she ought to be able to see Him in you, not only in the Bible."

I sat thinking silently, and a few moments later Mr. Owen came in, and we told him what we had been talking about. He was deeply interested, and asked whether Philippa had a Bible.

"No," I answered, "but I could buy her one for a birthday present. What would it cost? I've got 7s.[1]"

"A good print one would cost more than that," said Mr. Owen, "but I think Janet would like to

[1] A shilling is fourteen cents—Elaine had approximately one dollar.

help. Tell her about it in the morning, and you could go into town together and choose it."

I went up to bed feeling very happy and only just resisted the temptation to wake Janet there and then and tell her our plan. But I was very sleepy myself and hardly remembered laying my head on the pillow before I woke to find the room full of sunshine and Janet poking me to wake me up. She was delighted when I told her my idea, and promised to throw in every penny she had, but that only added up to 2s. 3½²., because she was an extremely generous little girl and was always giving presents.

We were spreading our joint collection on the table to count it properly, when Peter came in.

"What are you girls going to do with all that money?" he asked suspiciously. "Don't forget, we've got to save for Camp. I'm going to try and buy a map and a compass, so you'll have to help on other things."

"But it's for Philippa's Bible," explained Janet "and I really think it's more important than Camp, because Elaine has started telling her, and Daddy's going to give her the Scripture Union notes."

"Oh, I see," said Peter, scratching his head

²Approximately fifty cents.

thoughtfully. He was a very shy boy in some ways and never talked about his deepest thoughts, but I knew he read his Bible as faithfully as Janet and was keener than anyone about bringing boys along to his father's Bible Class on Sunday.

"Well, you don't seem to have much between you," he said suddenly and rather contemptuously, and turning on his heel he left the room.

"Oh dear!" said Janet, who adored her brother, "I'm afraid he's cross. After all, we did say we'd save up for Camp, but I thought there was still time for that. We've got all our pocket money for two months, and we can do some odd jobs."

She was interrupted by Peter's clattering feet, taking the stairs three steps at a time. He marched into the room and threw 5s.[3] on the table.

"Might as well get her a decent one while you're about it," he said gruffly. "And when you go to choose it, I'll come with you." He was gone before we could even say Thank You, slamming the door very hard behind him.

We set off early next morning on our bicycles, for the nearest town where Bibles could be bought was seven miles away. We went the back way through winding roads between buttercup fields, avoiding the trafficky crossroads. It was Whitsun

---

[3]About seventy-five cents.

holiday, and fine weather, and the town we knew would be crowded with holiday makers.

It was worse than we had even imagined, and we had the greatest difficulty in keeping together. We left our bicycles in a garage and fought our way through the enormous crowds outside Woolworth's. There was a traffic block in the road, and the Police seemed hot and bothered.

"Here we are," shouted Peter rather breathlessly, squeezing himself between two fat women with ice-cream cones, and trying to hold the way open for us. We had to shout, because the band on the front was making such a noise that we could hardly hear ourselves speak. But the bookshop was quieter than the street, and we made our way to the glass case where Bibles were kept and stood entranced. A kindly shop girl asked us which we wanted.

"We'd like to see them all in turn, please," said Peter grandly, "provided they don't cost more than 14s. 3½.[4] That is actually our limit."

The girl smiled and waited patiently, as for ten minutes we looked and argued and discussed and changed our minds. But in the end we all agreed on a beautiful cloth-bound one that cost 13s. 6d.[5] with large print and pictures.

[4]About two dollars.
[5]About one dollar and ninety-five cents.

"Good," said Peter with a sigh of relief, "ninepence halfpenny left! Now let's have an iced lolly each, and that leaves a halfpenny for Camp. Come on now, inch by inch, to that shop over there!"

We had reached the ice-cream stall and were standing in a doorway sucking noisily, when I suddenly saw it, and my heart seemed to miss a beat. I looked again. Yes, it was quite unmistakeable— the face that had haunted me for weeks, an ugly, unshaven face with wild, frightened eyes.

"Peter," I whispered, clutching hold of him so hard he dropped his ice. "Peter, it's him!"

"Who?" retorted Peter. "Look out, Elaine, my ice!"

"Never mind your ice, Peter," I breathed urgently. "Look, LOOK, there by the crossing! The man I saw in the Thomases' garden! Oh, Peter, do let's get away quick, he may see me!"

I cowered down in a doorway, but I was too late. At a sign from the policeman a crowd of people swarmed across the road, leaving a gap. The man turned suddenly, and his eyes held mine for a moment in a frightened stare of recognition. The next instant he had dived off into the crowds and disappeared up a side street.

"Quick!" shouted Peter, who in that startled moment had recaptured his ice and was now waving it above his head in his excitement. "There's a policeman, tell him!"

He plunged toward the policeman on point duty, tripping over a dog lead and pushing an angry lady into the arms of an astonished gentleman. "We've seen the thief who took the things from Mr. Thomas's house," he yelled, clutching hold of the blue sleeve, "he's just made off, but I expect you could catch him if you tried."

The policeman shook him off impatiently. "I don't care if you've seen the thief what rifled Buckingham Palace," he retorted with his eyes on the traffic. "I've got my job to do. If you've anything to report, you can go to the Station up Emrys Street."

He blew his whistle violently at a car that was doing the wrong thing, and Peter fought his way back to us.

"It's no good," he said disappointedly, "it would take us half an hour to get to Emrys Street in these crowds, and he could have got anywhere by then. There are buses leaving all the time. Oh, to think I got as near as that, and missed him!"

We moved into a side street and leaned dejectedly against the wall. "I don't think the Police take much notice of children, anyhow," went on Peter. "We'd better get home quick and tell Daddy.

He could always 'phone if he liked . . . and anyhow, one good thing, I've seen him myself now, and I should know him again *anywhere!*"

CHAPTER XVI

THE CHILD AT THE DOOR

THE SUMMER SPED BY and, without knowing it, I was changing as rapidly as the seasons round about me. To begin with, I was shooting up like a young tree, and Mrs. Owen was kept busy letting my frocks out at the waist and down at the hem. I had also really started to enjoy school and was working hard at lessons and games. And, more than that, I was beginning to realise what a beautiful world I lived in, and what wonderful things there were to see and hear and smell and discover all round me. It was as though my eyes had been opened, and to me some of the landmarks of that Summer were the foxgloves on Moelfre Hill, the smell of warm heather and new-mown hay on the uplands, and that early Sunday morning when Janet and I picked the first curly wild-rose buds in the lane leading down to the river.

I was learning more than school lessons, too.

Quite regularly, three times a week, I climbed the hill in the long light evenings after supper and sat for half an hour with Philippa. Sometimes Janet came too, and we always spent part of that time reading the Scripture Union portion and talking about it, for Philippa's Bible had become her dearest possession. All through her illness she had had nothing much to think about but herself, and she was tired and bored and unhappy. Even her storybooks bothered her, because they were all about strong, healthy children who ran about and had adventures. But the Bible opened up a wonderful new world to her. It was all about sick people who were healed, sad people who were comforted, tired people who found rest, lost sheep that were found, and sinful people who were forgiven; while always in the midst of them, shining from every page, was the Saviour Who called them to come and in Whose Presence was fulness of joy.

"I do love Him," said Philippa suddenly one night as we sat together in the Summer twilight. It had rained that day, and the air was fragrant with washed flowers folding their petals. "I wish I really belonged to Him, like you. But He hasn't made me walk yet, and I sometimes wonder if He really listens to me."

"You could belong to Him as I do," I said simply. "But when I tell you, you never seem to understand. I'm going to ask Auntie to come. She'll tell you. She's ever so good at explaining things. I'll bring her before we go to Camp."

Philippa's face brightened. "Yes, do," she answered. "I like Mrs. Owen. I'd like to make certain before you go to Camp, because I shan't see you for a whole ten days. Still, my Daddy's coming home after that, so that's something to look forward to."

Plans for Camp had forged ahead. Peter and his father had bicycled over one day and found a farmhouse near a lake that would take Mrs. Owen, Robin, and Lucy, let us camp by the water's edge, and provide us with milk and eggs. Then my mother had covered herself with glory by sending us three pounds towards the equipment, and we'd bought ground sheets. The Boy Scouts had lent us two tents, and we'd collected sacks to stuff with straw as mattresses and sewn up old blankets for sleeping-bags. Peter had spent three Saturdays bringing in the hay and had earned his map and compass, and Mrs. Owen was laying up stores of provisions on the top shelf of the kitchen cupboard. We were beginning to talk Camp all day and dream it all night.

By the time I had reached the garden gate, I knew that something very exciting had happened, for I could hear the noise quite a long way away —loud hurrahs from Peter and Janet and excited squeaks from the younger members of the family. I dashed up the path and flung myself unhesitatingly into the scrum that raged round Mr. Owen, for I felt myself a member of the family now.

"What's happened?" I shouted, "Tell me quick!"

"A car for the holiday!" yelled Peter. "Mr. Jones is so grateful to Daddy for making Mrs. Jones better that he's lending him his car for August. We shall be able to explore everywhere now, and Mummy and the babies will be able to come too."

"Steady, Pete," broke in Mr. Owen, "I'm not a doctor."

But we all knew about poor Mrs. Jones, whose precious baby, her first, had died quite suddenly. We had taken the first narcissi to lay on the tiny grave one sunny day in April. The poor mother had nearly gone out of her mind, and the doctor could do nothing but suggest that she should go into a Home. It was only Mr. Owen's prayers and patient daily visits, leading her back step by step to the Source of comfort, that saved her reason. She was now up and about again, a new woman, visiting and comforting others who were in sorrow. No wonder Mr. Jones was grateful.

It really was wonderful news, for the mountain buses were few and far between, and Lucy seemed to need nearly as much luggage as the Camp. Now we could take over the gear in advance, and then come back for Mrs. Owen and the babies. Besides, we could reach the foot of the great mountains by car and do some real climbing in the day and get back to Camp at night. Peter had even produced a climbing-rope.

School exams claimed our attention for the last fortnight of term, but the great day really was approaching slowly, for we were to leave on the second day of the Summer holidays. Mrs. Owen was very busy looking out our clothes and preparing the house for the minister who was coming to take the Church services while we were away, so I waited till Sunday to ask her about Philippa. She said she would come up directly after supper and leave Blodwen and Janet to put the little ones to bed. So that evening we set out together hand in hand, and when we reached the grassy slope under the old beeches Mrs. Owen stopped and sat down on the mossy roots.

"Let's pray before we go in," she said, and I sat down beside her and closed my eyes, and she asked God to show Philippa the way and bring her to Himself. Then we entered the garden and found Mrs. Thomas and Philippa sitting together at the open window.

Mrs. Thomas was very pleased to see Mrs. Owen, and I thought she'd never stop talking. But she was always glad enough to slip off and get on with some work, while someone else took a turn at entertaining her daughter, so after about ten minutes she said she'd run out and see about supper, and we were left alone.

Philippa turned eagerly to Mrs. Owen. "Good," she said. "You've come! I've been waiting every day. Did Elaine tell you?"

"Yes," answered Mrs. Owen, coming straight to the point, for she was always a little bit nervous of staying long away from her babies. "You are worried, aren't you? because you've asked God to make you walk properly, and He hasn't, and you can't understand why."

Philippa nodded. Her eyes were fixed on Mrs. Owen's face as though she was listening to some wonderful secret.

"I think it's like this," said Mrs. Owen, speaking very slowly, and staring out into the still, scented garden. "Supposing a ragged, homeless boy came to my door and asked me for five shillings. I could give him five shillings and send him away, or I could do something far better. I could say to him, 'I'm not going to give you five shillings, but I'm going to take you into my home and love you and wash you clean and care for you, and make you my own little child' If I said that, do you think that little boy would go on worrying about his five shillings? He'd know that I loved him enough to give him every single thing he needed."

"Is the five shillings like my legs?" asked Philippa. She was a very quick child in some ways.

"A little bit," answered Mrs. Owen. "You've asked the Lord Jesus to give you strong legs, and He's looking down at you and saying, 'Philippa, I've got something far better for you than that. I love you, and I want you to be My own little girl. I want to save you from all your crossness and sadness and selfishness, and I want to make you happy'. Of course, later on He may give you strong legs as well, and you can go on asking Him, but first of all He wants to teach you that if you belong to Him you can be happy, wonderfully happy, even lying here on this couch. Has Elaine showed you her text in the front of her Bible?"

"Yes," answered Philippa promptly, "I can say

it. 'Thou wilt show me the path of life. In Thy Presence is fulness of joy'."

"Good," said Mrs. Owen. "Do you see what it means? It means that when we come to the Lord Jesus we tell Him that we are willing for Him to choose our path of life, because He knows best. And that means that if He sends illness or sorrow or disappointment, we shan't grumble. We shall know that He is close beside us, and we shall be happy, because, you know, Philippa, happiness doesn't really depend on what you've got or where you are. Real, true, lasting happiness cames from living close to the Lord Jesus and being like Him."

Philippa said nothing. She often turned things over for a long time in her mind before coming to any decisions, and anyhow, a few minutes later Mrs. Thomas came back and switched on the light and begged us to stay to supper. Mrs. Owen jumped to her feet.

"I really must get back and see what the family is doing," she cried. "They are all wild with excitement because Mr. Jones has offered to lend my husband a car in order to take us all to Camp. The Joneses are going to stay with his parents, and they've got a car already, so they were just going to leave theirs in the garage. Isn't it wonderful! I can't tell you how I was dreading carting all the Camp gear and the babies on the bus, and dragging them all miles up a mountain the other end."

I glanced at Philippa. There was a lonely, wistful little look on her face that filled me with pity. I suddenly had a marvellous idea.

"Auntie," I shouted, "It's not very far with a car! Couldn't Uncle come one day and fetch Mrs. Thomas and Philippa to see the Camp and come and have tea with us? Oh, Auntie, do say yes!"

Philippa's face had gone pink with excitement, and her eyes were shining. Both mothers looked quite alarmed for a moment.

"We'll have to ask my husband," said Mrs. Owen. "As a matter of fact, if you don't think it's too tiring for Philippa, I should say it was a splendid idea."

"So should I," said Philippa quickly. "Mummy, if you'll say Yes, I'll never be cross again!"

We all burst out laughing at this, and Mrs. Owen and I hurried home through the dusk. It was high time, too, for things had not gone too successfully during our absence, and Blodwen and Janet looked ruffled and heated. Lucy was screaming, and Robin, for no reason that anyone could discover, had dropped his socks into Monday morning's porridge. Johnny, who had wanted to stay up till his mother returned, had hidden in the linen cupboard and was just being dragged out struggling by one leg. Only good little Frances had gone quietly up to bed, and she was waiting to come down again the moment her father came in.

Mrs. Owen had the situation in hand in a few moments. She listened to Blodwen's complaints, hushed Lucy, spanked Robin, kissed Frances, and quenched Johnny, and put the kettle on for a cup of tea.

"I should have gone to-morrow," she remarked peacefully, when we were all sitting round the kitchen table. "I forgot that children are always naughtier on Sunday than on any other night of the week. Now, here come Daddy and Pete. Let's pour out."

Mr. Owen and Peter came in from Church as hungry as though we'd never had early supper at all, so we all started again on tea and buns. It was a pleasant evening, and everyone thoroughly approved my plan of fetching Philippa over for the day, and we should have gone on chatting all night if Mrs. Owen hadn't chased us up to bed.

Before lying down, I stood at the open window a few minutes and leaned far out. The warm Summer darkness smelt of stocks and snapdragons and lavender, and an owl hooted softly from the beeches. In Philippa's house a light was still burning, and I wondered what she was doing. Was she still standing outside begging for gifts, or had she looked up into the Face of the Giver and entered in through the door into the light and safety of the Father's House?

CHAPTER XVII

THE CAMP BY THE LAKE

THE GREAT MORNING dawned at last, as all great mornings will, although they seem so long in coming. Mr. Owen set out with us four older children and the tents at crack of dawn to pitch Camp, and then he was going back to fetch Mrs. Owen and the little ones after dinner.

It was a perfect blue morning, and we travelled by the narrow back lanes dipping down to the river between hedges tangled with honeysuckle and late wild roses. Here and there were gates set in the hedge through which one had glimpses of high hills rising up on the other side of the valley, and sometimes we dipped into tunnels of trees, their thick green foliage interlaced and shutting out the sky. We sang for miles, leaning far out of the car windows filling our lungs with the scented wind. The dew still lay on the fields when we started, and the spiders' webs shone like silver.

We left the lanes after a time and joined a winding road that ran along the river bank for a few miles and then began to climb toward the horizon; and then suddenly we reached the top of the hill, and Mr. Owen stopped the car abruptly and said, "Look!"

I gave a little gasp, for never before had I seen the great mountains close. Now they stretched out in front of us as far as the eye could see, a shimmering range of heathery slopes and proud rocky summits. Peter jumped on to the footboard and reeled off the names—Moel Siabod, the Glyders, Snowdon, the Cannedds, fierce, jagged little Tryfan. And we knew that hidden away in the misty folds of their dips and valleys were the Lakes. Peter leaped back into the car and prodded his father in the back.

"Go on, Daddy," he shouted, "let's get there!"

So we raced down the hill and into the last little town, where pink and blue and yellow cottages stand in rows on the outskirts, and where in olden days they made the harps that filled all Wales with their wild music; then over an old stone bridge designed, so Mr. Owen told us, by a famous architect called Inigo Jones, and then we had left civilisation behind us and were speeding towards the steep forest-clad wall of mountain that seemed to rise sheer ahead of us. Only ten more minutes, and we left the last proper road and turned up a steep stony path that climbed through larch woods, with a stream foaming down over mossy boulders on our right.

"Will the car really go up here?" asked Janet, clutching the back of the seat nervously. "And what shall we do if we meet another car?"

"I can't think," replied Mr. Owen. "It would be just too bad!" He pulled down into bottom gear and hooted his horn warningly as we twisted round the corners. But no one else was on the road that morning, and we came out above the forests on to the level mountain track, where seas of heather rolled away on either side of us and the rocks rose up to the peaks wherever we looked.

We were breathless with excitement now, for we knew that in a few minutes we should see the spot that Peter had described to us. And then we bumped round the corner of a jutting crag, and there in front of us, clear as green glass, with the shadows of the hills reflected in its depths, lay the lake.

Mr. Owen stopped the car, and once again we were silent for a moment, and I at least thought I had never seen anything so beautiful before. It was so still and so long. It lay in a green cup of the mountains flanked on the far side by steep larch woods that grew right down to the margin of the water. On the near side the rushes grew in the shallows, and the hill rose gently, clothed in heather and harebells and spongy bog moss. Now and then a gull dipped and ruffled the surface with its wings, but otherwise I couldn't see a ripple. I felt as though I had reached an enchanted country, where everything seemed to have fallen asleep.

"Oh, Daddy, let's bathe," squealed Johnny, recovering his astonished senses. "Look, there's a little beach! Couldn't we make Camp there?"

"No," replied Mr. Owen. "We've got to get to the other end to the farmhouse. Look, there's a little white road along the edge of the lake. We'll get the tents up and Camp fixed, and then we'll have a dip before dinner. We won't bother about cooking to-day—just corned beef and bread and butter and plums and lemonade; then I can get back early for Mummy."

We drove along the little track by the edge of the water, and very soon we caught sight of Mrs. Davies's farm—a whitewashed building surrounded by a low stone wall and hidden by a spinney of mountain ash trees. There was a sheepfold and a cowshed to one side of it, and a wire run for chickens, and a spring of clear water splashing into a stone trough in front of the door. Mrs. Davies heard us coming and ran out to meet us. She was a neat dark little woman with rosy cheeks and bright black eyes, with a little girl clinging to her apron, and a large sheepdog capering round her.

"A little friend for Francie," said Mr. Owen, waving at the child.

"And a little friend for Cadwaller," said Johnny, whistling the sheepdog.

We tumbled out of the car, and Mr. Owen greeted her in Welsh, which pleased her, for her English was shaky, and the little girl knew none. She pointed out the driest spot for the Camp site and helped us carry up the things. It was a tufty little grass platform with heather sloping away in front and a screen of small stunted oaks behind.

We set to work in good earnest, laying the ground sheets and hammering in the tent pegs, and then we went to Mrs. Davies, and she took us round to the barn to stuff our mattresses, for she had promised to give us all the straw we needed. It was cool and dim and clean and smelt of cows and new-mown hay, and in a partition in the corner was a tiny black-and-white calf, very weak and wobbly, peeping out from behind its mother.

We dragged the mattresses up the hill and spread out the sleeping bags, and Peter and Johnny dug a banked-up hole in the hillside, which they lined with canvas for tins and provisions. Then we carried big stones up from the lake and built the Camp fireplace. Our firewood we were going to store in the barn, for the rain comes suddenly and swiftly over the Welsh mountains.

"We'll build a whopping Camp fire to welcome Mummy to-night," said Pete. "We'll all collect wood while you go and fetch her. Now come on, let's have a swim before dinner."

We'd changed in two minutes and raced barefoot over the springy grass to the pebbly stretch of mud among the rushes that Johnny had already christened "the bathing beach." Here the ground sloped gently, so it would be safe even for the little ones, and Peter, Janet, and Johnny were already good swimmers. They made straight for the clear green depths and swam out with their father, leaving me splashing in the shallows.

Then, hungry as hunters, we sat down to piles of bread and butter and corned beef and a large enamel jug of lemonade. We were still sitting munching in contented silence when Mr. Owen glanced at his watch and jumped up.

"I must go and fetch Mummy," he said, "and

we shan't be back till about five o'clock. You can collect firewood and explore around, but don't get lost and, remember, no one is to go near the lake or light a fire until we get back."

We all nodded, our mouths being too full to speak, and Mr. Owen jumped into the car and went bumping off along the stony lakeside track. We looked round with renewed interest, for it was rather exciting being left on our own, even if Mrs. Davies was only fifty yards down the hill.

"You girls, wash up," said Peter, draining off his lemonade, "and then let's lay an enormous bonfire for to-night. And then let's go to the other end of the lake and follow the stream and see where it goes to. It says on my map that there's another big lake over the other side of the mountain with a stream flowing down that joins this one. If we found the place where they met, we should know our way up to it another day."

We tidied up and dug a deep hole for tins and rubbish, and then scattered to collect firewood. I climbed to a little copse of larches and firs on the crest of our ridge and almost forgot my errand in looking about me. I had never before been in such wild, rolling scenery. I turned my back on the lake, and mile after mile of heathery moorland lay in front of me, broken by rocks and mountain trees, fold upon fold of high hills backed by the distant grandeur of mountains, and not a living creature to be seen anywhere.

"Come on," shouted Peter's voice from the Camp far below me, "you've hardly got any, and we want to start soon."

I began picking up twigs in a great hurry and managed to produce quite a reasonable armful in the next few minutes. We'd collected a big pile between us, and after paying another call on the black-and-white calf and some further conversation with Mrs. Davies we started along the edge of the lake, feeling like a party of explorers setting out to discover unknown territory. Peter carried the map and the compass in a leather wallet over his shoulder. The sky had clouded since morning. It was cool and very silent.

We reached the end of the lake where it narrowed into a rushing white stream that tumbled over the edge of the plateau and went hurrying down a deep rocky stream-bed. We had our sandals off in a moment and scrambled down the steep banks, leaping from boulder to boulder. Now and then we slipped on the wet stones and went splashing up to our knees in a foaming pool, but we did not mind that. We went joyfully on until the stream ran under a tunnel of trees, and here it was quieter and greener, and long ferns dipped to the water.

"Don't forget we've got to get back," said Janet, pausing. "We musn't be late for Mummy."

"Well, the trees end just ahead," called back Peter. "We're coming out on to a rocky, stony sort of place. Just come out into the open and have a look round, and then we'll go back."

We waded on, and as the trees gave way to grey sky, we found ourselves in a desolate place indeed. It must have been an old stone quarry once, for piles of broken stones, unclothed by foliage, rose around us, and just in front of us were the blackened walls of an old, roofless, stone building.

"Looks as though it had been burned," said Peter thoughtfully. "Give me a leg up, someone, and let's see inside."

"I think we ought to go home," said Janet firmly. "I don't like that house, Pete. In fact, I don't like this place at all. It's sort of ghostly."

I looked round and shivered a little. The piles of slag hid the countryside, and to our left rose a wall of jagged black rock dividing the two valleys that nursed their hidden lakes. But just below the old quarry the two streams met, and the air was full of the sound of angry rushing water.

Peter was wading through the mass of dock and

nettle that surrounded the ruin and had hoisted himself up on the sill. "I say," he called back excitedly, "it's got all sorts of rooms in it, and someone has made a camp fire—there are black stones and ashes and an old saucepan. I can't see into the other rooms, but one is still roofed over, and the windows stuffed up with rags. I believe someone lives there. I'm going to try the door!"

He jumped down into the nettles, stinging his legs badly, and picked his way down to the door. It was jammed and stuck, but Peter went at it with his shoulder, and it burst open so suddenly that he fell forward. He got up quickly and backed out, rather frightened, and stood hesitating.

"Shall I go in?" he asked. "Supposing there's someone in there?"

"I should think he'd have come out by now," said Johnny rather sensibly. Then he hopped over the nettles and stood in the doorway.

"I'll go in," he said gaily, "I'm not frightened."

He skipped into the ruin, poking his inquisitive little nose into one derelict room after another. Then he came tiptoeing back, his eyes round with excitement.

"Someone does live there," he whispered. "There's a mattress with nice blankets and some plates and cups, and a box and an old rug on the floor."

"Oh, Peter," I whispered, "let's go home! Supposing they come, they'll be awfully cross if they find us in their house, and we shall never hear them till they are right on top of us, the stream's making such a row."

"Well, I'd just like to have a squint," said Peter uncertainly. "Johnny, you climb on that slag heap and keep a look-out."

Nimble little Johnny was up in a moment and down again as quickly.

"There's a man coming up beside the stream," he squeaked, "and he's got a sack over his back and a dead rabbit in his hand! Come ON, everybody, run!" and Johnny was away into the tunnel of trees, leaping from boulder to boulder with Peter and Janet just behind him and me slipping and stumbling and splashing along in the rear. On we went, breathless and wet, with bruised, cold feet and aching legs; nor did we feel safe till we reached the quiet pocket of the hills and the grey levels of the lake.

"There's the car!" shouted Janet, waving her sandals wildly above her head, and the next moment we were all racing along barefoot beside it, with the joyful faces of Frances, Robin, Lucy, and

Cadwaller filling the windows, and Mrs. Owen calling out greetings; and although none of us would have confessed it, never before in our lives had we been so pleased to see them.

CHAPTER XVIII

PHILIPPA'S DAY

THE SUN SEEMED TO COME OUT as Mrs. Owen struggled out of the car, her arms full of Lucy and a bursting paper bag of home-made buns. We all flung ourselves upon her, and the rest of the evening was an uproarious success. Mr. Owen had the fire going and the kettle boiling in no time, and we sat round, warming our chilly legs and drying our wet skirts and trousers. Soon we were all eating buns and drinking enamel mugfuls of hot, sweet tea that tasted of wood smoke and condensed milk, and discussing what we should have for supper.

"I think we'll have fried eggs and bacon to-night as a treat," said Mrs. Owen, "and finish up with cocoa and biscuits round the camp fire. Perhaps Mrs. Davies and her little girl will join us. Now, let's unpack the provisions, and—oh, Elaine, I quite forgot! There's a letter for you from your mother. It came by the mid-day post."

She handed me a thin letter with a French
stamp on it, and a funny little cold feeling of fear
seemed to rise up inside me, for Mummy hardly
ever wrote letters. She sent me postcards every
week or so, but they only said, "How are you?
Cheerio!" or something like that. I turned away
from the others who were all digging in the pro-
vision box and ran up the thill to the coppice
where I'd gathered firewood and sat down on the
roots of the larch tree, crumpling the letter up in
my hand. It was silly to feel afraid, for the last
time she'd written she sent three pounds for Camp.

I tore the letter open and read it through several times, because at first I really could not take
it in, and yet I'd known all along that it must come
one day. The man Mummy worked for was
coming home in the Autumn. Mummy would keep
on with her job, but she would find a home for us
both in London. "You had better stay and finish
your school term," she wrote, "but you will be back
with me for the Christmas holidays, and we'll find
a school for you in London after that. I've missed
you so much, and it will be lovely to be together
again."

The Christmas holidays! Janet had told me all
about them: the frosty evenings when they sang
carols and left little gifts all round the village by

lantern light; the tobogganing and the opening of
stockings on Christmas morning: the Sunday
School party in the hall, when Mr. Owen dressed
up as Father Christmas—and now I should miss
it all.

I gazed down at the Camp. It was nearly sunset; and the crags stood up black against a prim-
rose sky, reflected in the still waters of the lake.
Peter and Johnny were dragging an enormous log
up from the barn, and Janet was squatting over a
saucepan doing something in the cooking line.
Frances stood alone on the little beach with her
back to everyone, a tiny, fairy figure held by the
beauty of the light on the water. No! I could not
leave them. They were my brothers and sisters
now. Surely Mrs. Owen would understand and
help me to explain to Mummy. Of course, I wanted
to see Mummy sometimes, and I would not mind
going to London occasionally, and she could come
and visit me in Wales. But my home was here in
the country with the wide skies and the changing
seasons and the children I'd learned to love.

My mind went back over the past few months.
How selfish and miserable I'd been at first, and
how I'd hated it! Yet somehow I'd been drawn in.
What was it, I wondered, that bound us all together and made us such a strong family circle? I

did not really understand at the moment, but I
was beginning to realise even then that the centre
of that home was the open Bible by whose pre-
cepts we were daily taught to live—that old, tried
Book that taught children to honour and obey
their parents and to love one another, and to
recognise life's true values. Who would go on
teaching me in London? How could I go on being
a Christian all by myself?

"Come on, Elaine," shouted Peter impatiently.
"We're just going to fry the bacon. Everyone has
got to sit down with a plate."

A delicious smell came floating up, and I went
down to join the family. Mrs. Owen pushed
Johnny out of the way and made a place for me,
and I snuggled comfortably against her. Perhaps she guessed what was in my letter.

Supper was a great success, and afterwards we
piled wood on the fire and made a blaze that lit
up the dark mountains all round and made rosy
reflections in the black lake. Mrs. Davies, Eiluned,
and Tudor, the sheepdog, joined us for cocoa
and biscuits, and we sang camp fire songs till we
were hoarse. Then by the light of the dying flames
Mr. Owen opened his Bible. Just below us we
could hear the soft bleating of the flock huddled
in the fold.

"And when He putteth forth His own sheep, He goeth before them, and the sheep follow Him: for they know His voice," read Mr. Owen, and as we sat listening, the moon rose over the far end of the valley flooding the lake with silver light. And we slept with the tent flaps thrown right back, so that its beams could shine down on us all night long.

Every day in Camp brought fresh delights. We rose in the cool dawning and bathed in the lake before breakfast. Peter was in charge of the fire, and Janet and I were the cooks, with Mrs. Owen giving advice. Sometimes we went on expeditions and climbed the mountains, and sometimes we just explored the near hills or messed about round the farm. And when the rain and mists came sweeping over the mountains, we played and turned somersaults in the barn, and on wet evenings Mrs. Davies made us welcome in her kitchen, which we loved. It was large and low with an uneven stone floor and a huge fireplace that took up most of one side of the wall. There were shining copper-coloured kettles, too, in which we could see our faces distorted to funny shapes, and queer old tapestries and samplers hung on the walls. It was altogether an exceedingly snug place on rainy nights, when the thunder broke over the crags and the wind whipped the lake into little white waves. We used to undress in Mrs. Owen's room when bedtime came, and dash up the dark slope in the storm and dive into our sleeping-bags.

One cloudless blue day we climbed Snowdon, and another day Mr. Owen took us roped up the steep side of Tryfan, and we felt ourselves accomplished mountaineers. With the help of Peter's map we discovered every lake hidden away in the secret folds of the hills and scaled every rocky heathery peak. I was becoming as brown as a berry and as strong as a mountain pony, and I sometimes wondered what my mother would think of me, if she saw me.

But to me the great event of the holiday was Philippa's visit, and on Saturday morning, long before the others were awake, I wriggled out of my sleeping-bag and crept to the door of the tent to look at the weather. It was still very early, but the sky behind the mountains was pearly blue, and the morning star was paling over the highest crag. A dawn wind came sighing up the valley, ruffling the dark waters of the lake and bowing the rushes. Down in the fold the sheep stirred restlessly in their sleep, and Cadwaller, in the lee of our tent, lifted his head and sniffed. "It's going to be a beautiful day," I thought to myself, shivering a

little. "There isn't a cloud to be seen." I pulled my
blanket round my shoulders and watched the sky
grow brighter and brighter behind the rocks. Two
gulls soared up from among the reeds on the edge
of the water, and I could see the light shining on
their pure wings. And because I was too excited
to feel sleepy, I stayed there watching until at last
the sun appeared through a green dip in the hills,
and the grass all round me turned silver and the
waters of the lake turned gold.

"Oh, wake up, Janet," I said impatiently, unable
to contain myself any longer. "Come and bathe!
The water's all shiny." But Janet only grunted and
disappeared far down her sleeping-bag, leaving
me to the company of Cadwaller.

Everything to my impatient fancy seemed to
move slowly that morning. The boys wouldn't get
up, and when they did no one could find the
porridge saucepan. However, after much searching someone noticed Robin crouching on the
bathing beach, playing his favourite game of boats,
and the saucepan bobbing about some way from
land. Peter had to swim out and fetch it, and then
the porridge wouldn't boil, and Lucy wouldn't eat
her plateful, and Cadwaller rushed off with the
teacloth, which delayed the washing up. In any
case, no one seemed in a hurry except me, and at

last I could bear it no longer. I rushed up to Mr. Owen, who was merely sitting in the sun listening to a story by Frances, and asked him what time he was thinking of fetching Philippa.

"Philippa?" said Mr. Owen calmly, glancing at his watch. "Why, yes, she was coming out to dinner to-day, wasn't she? I'd better start now while the weather's fine, and get her out early. It may cloud over later."

He got up and glanced at the car. "We'll leave the whole back seat for Philippa," he said, "but there's room for three in the front. Like to come with me, Elaine? It would be fun for Philippa to have you on the way back."

I was thrilled, and rushed off to get tidy. Frances, green with envy, ran after her father.

"Daddy, Daddy!" she whispered beseechingly, "will you invite me when you take her back? Because you did want to hear the end of that story, didn't you?"

"Terribly!" answered Mr. Owen, stooping down to her. "This afternoon, Francie, we'll come back all by ourselves and have tea in a teashop on the way. Don't tell!"

Frances' small freckled face reminded me of the moment when the sun came over the crags— it lit up so suddenly with such radiance of joy.

She deserved a treat, for she was not quite big
enough to climb the mountains, yet it was always
a bitter disappointment to get left behind. She
would go and sit quietly by the lake, staring out
over the water and squeezing her hands together,
swallowing down her sorrow til we were out of
sight.

I thoroughly enjoyed the drive, and when we
arrived, I rushed ahead to see if Philippa was
ready. She had been ready for ages, sitting at the
window, and within five minutes we were off
again, Philippa stretched out on the back seat, and
me, sandwiched between Mr. Owen and Mrs.
Thomas, leaning over the back to talk to her. Of
course there was an awful lot to tell, and I chattered on without stopping, for Philippa wanted
to know exactly what we'd been doing every moment of every day. So I rattled on about camp
fires and tents, calves and sheep, lakes and mountains, climbing, bathing, and exploring, and she
lay and listened with a longing look on her face,
like someone gazing at an enchanted country
through locked gates.

"And what have you been doing?" I asked when
we were nearly there.

"Nothing much," answered Philippa, quite cheerfully, "just sitting!"

I glanced at her in surprise, for she was not speaking in her usual whiny, self-pitying voice. She looked at me straight in the eyes and pursed up her lips to whisper. "I want to tell you something when we are alone," she breathed mysteriously, and I nodded and winked, for I liked secrets. Then I forgot all about it, for we were climbing the lane that led up to the lake, and in a few minutes we should drive round the jutting spur of rock that narrowed the way into the kingdom.

"Oh," cried Philippa, "there they are, and look, there's a lake . . . oh, Elaine, what a beautiful place!"

Mr. Owen put on the brakes rather suddenly, for the five children had come to meet us and were standing with joined hands right across the road, sunburnt, laughing, and dishevelled. Robin was in the middle, barefoot and prancing, delighted to be out with his elders and betters. Then with a wild whoop they dropped hands and were off, pelting over the springy turf in an effort to race the car. But Mr. Owen pressed on the accelerator, and in a few moments we'd left them far behind, and Philippa and I stuck our heads out of the window and yelled with triumph.

There was a couch of bracken and heather ar-

ranged on the hillside for Philippa, and Mr.
Owen carried her up over the rough ground and
laid her down by the camp fire. Dinner was almost
ready, and it was a real feast for the occasion—
fried sausages, potatoes baked in the ashes, split
open and stuffed with butter, and a huge plum
pie made by Mrs. Davies. We finished up with
smoky campfire tea, after which we all felt very
full and lay about on the warm turf sucking
toffees produced by Philippa, while Mrs. Owen
read *The Wind in the Willows* aloud to us.

She had only finished one chapter, when Mrs.
Thomas pointed rather anxiously to the far end
of the lake. A strange white mist was stealing
through a gap in the hills like a thief with cold
hands, wreathing about the lower slopes in ragged
wisps. Already the clump of larches that guarded
the entrance looked dim and ghostly, and a chill
seemed to be creeping over the face of the sun.

CHAPTER XIX

A SHOCK AND A MEETING

I THINK we should be going home," said Mrs. Thomas. "I don't want Philippa to get cold. It's been such a lovely, lovely treat for us both."

"Oh, Mummy," pleaded Philippa, "just wait five minutes. The mist's coming ever so slowly, and I want to talk to Elaine for a minute. I shan't see her for another whole five days."

"Very well, darling," said Mrs. Thomas, "just five minutes. I'm going with Francie and Robin to see the baby calf."

Peter, Janet, and Johnny went off to do the washing up in the lake, and I sprawled on the grass beside Philippa's bracken nest. She was bursting with her secret and wasted no time coming to the point.

"Elaine," she began, "do you remember what Mrs. Owen said about begging at the door or going in?"

"Yes," I answered. "Of course I do. Have you gone in, Phil?"

"Yes, I think so," replied Philippa rather shyly. "I thought about it so much. And one night, instead of saying 'Please make my legs better,' I said, 'Please can I come inside and be Your own little girl?' And from that day I've had a sort of feeling that I might be happy even if my legs didn't get any better. I've asked Jesus to change me and to stop me being selfish and cross, and now I keep on having new ideas about what I could do. It's rather fun. I'd never thought of them before, because I used to think there was nothing nice to do if you were a cripple; only I'm longing for you to come home and help me with them."

"What sort of ideas?" I asked, deeply interested.

"Oh, things like helping Mummy, and making things for people," said Philippa, "and seeing how long I can go without grumbling and bothering over my lessons. I haven't time to explain now, but I keep on thinking about your text. If it was my path of life to be a cripple, it says I could still be happy, doesn't it?"

"Yes," I said firmly. "Fulness of joy, anywhere, if we are walking the path of life with Jesus. Uncle has explained it to me lots of times."

"Philippa," called Mrs. Thomas, "we really must be going, or we shall be caught in the mist."

And the next moment Mr. Owen had bounded up the slope and picked up Philippa in his arms. There was just time to show her the calf on the way down, and then she was lifted into the car. Frances, in the seventh heaven of delight, peeped out from between the grown-ups in the middle of the front seat.

"Can I ride on the running-board to the far end of the lake?" shouted Peter, jumping up.

"Me too!" I cried, clinging to the window on the other side. It would be fun to have another two minutes with Philippa.

"Right," said Mr. Owen, "just to the top of the lake. No, Johnny, you another time, three's too heavy."

The car started up, driving slowly along the lake side, and we clung on laughing and chattering, yet shivering a little, for we were driving straight into that creeping white mist, and it seemed to wrap us round with its cold dank fingers. I was not sorry when we reached the trees at the top of the lane and jumped off. It was going to be an evening for Mrs. Davies's kitchen and the cosy fireside.

Peter stood looking round. "I've never been in

such a thick mist before," he said. "I can't see the lake at all. And here's someone coming down that other path—look, Elaine, a man! I wonder where he's going. Not many people come this way."

We had stepped back into the shelter of the jutting out rock, and our voices were muffled by the mist. He could not see us, but we could see him quite clearly. He had a tinker's bag slung over his shoulder, that clattered a little as though he was carrying pots and pans, and the moment I set eyes on him, I knew him. A chill ran through me that was nothing to do with the mist. Peter stood rigid and uncertain beside me; he too had caught a glimpse of that wild, unshaven face under the slouch hat.

"Elaine," he whispered, backing behind the rock, "is it him?"

I nodded.

"Certain sure?"

"Absolutely certain."

"Well then, this time we mustn't miss him!" Peter's eyes were burning with high adventure. "He can't see us in that mist, and we can track him by that funny clatter and his boots on the stones. We must follow him, Elaine, and see where he goes. Come on!"

There was nothing for it but to follow, for I was

far too frightened to go home alone; also I did not want to desert Peter. So I set off behind him, shivering with cold and fear. The man did not go down the lane. He turned off to the left across the boggy uplands which made our quest far more difficult and dangerous, for there were no covering trees, and we had to keep a good distance away. We could just see his dim, shambling figure striding along, and we knew that if he turned round, he would certainly see us.

He was walking very fast, for he was wearing big boots that squelched through the mud and bog moss, but for me in my small sandals it was much harder going. Twice I sank right down into black water over my ankles and, to my terror, Peter seemed to be getting ahead of me, and I dared not call lest the man should hear and turn round.

Thicker and thicker grew the mist; it seemed to be building white walls all around us. I began to panic and to run wildly to catch up Peter, but it was treacherous ground to run on. I caught my foot in a clump of thick heather and fell headlong. Just for a moment I was too stunned to move, and when at length I scrambled up again, I was quite alone in a white, silent world. Peter and the man had completely disappeared.

Well, he couldn't be far ahead. Surely all I had to do was to run fast for a few minutes, and Peter's sturdy figure would loom up in front of me. But I forgot that we were following no road, and I'd lost all sense of direction. He might have gone anywhere, and the more I ran, the further away from him I might be going, out into the lonely night to be swallowed up by the thick darkness and the mist.

There was only one thing to do, and that was to turn right about and try to find my way home again. So I turned round and trotted off, shivering and crying, in the direction I thought we had come from. My shins were bruised and scratched, and my clothes drenched with mud and mist, but surely the lake couldn't be far off! If I went on long enough, I was bound to come to the valley, and then I could track my way up by the stream. If only Mr. Owen were there, he could come and look for me, but once he and Frances got away together, there was no knowing what time they'd be back, and it was after three o'clock when they left—probably not till nightfall and, anyhow, day or night made little difference in this eerie gloom. I stretched out my hand in front of me and found I could hardly see it.

I suppose I walked for hours, and I realise now

that I must have gone round and round in circles. I was almost too tired to feel frightened any more, and at last I sat down hopelessly on a little rock and gave myself up for lost. There was a queer new quality creeping into the mist now, too, the quality of darkness. The ghostly white was changing into grey, and I knew that night was falling over the hills. I wondered dully what had happened to Peter, and I tried to think what to do next. There seemed no point in stumbling along through the bog moss for ever, and yet, if I sat still on that wet rock, I was sure I should freeze to death. My mind drifted back over the events of the day. It seemed years and years since I'd sat on the sunny slope with Philippa. What had we talked about?

> *"Thou wilt show me the Path of Life . . .*
> *in Thy Presence is fulness of joy."*

It wasn't the Path of Life I wanted just then, it was the path back to Camp. It was the first time since being lost that I had been able to collect my ideas, for I had been quite stupid with panic and cold before. But now into my weary, numbed brain there stole a new thought. Was the Lord Jesus still there beside me in the mist? Was I still in His Presence? If so, why was I so dreadfully afraid?

"Show me the path, Lord Jesus," I whispered, and the very Name seemed to warm and strengthen me and give me new courage. I got up and went on walking, not knowing where I was going, but with a strong feeling of being led. For nearer than the wet clinging darkness and the deep loneliness was the sense of the Presence of the Good Shepherd, Who long ago, I remembered, had gone out on the mountains to seek for one lost sheep, and how much more now for a lost child? A new peace stole into my heart, and I suddenly felt safe.

Once again I could not say how long I walked. Sometimes I called out, but my voice sounded so small in the inky blackness that I gave it up. I think I was jogging along half-asleep, conscious of strange pains in my limbs, but nothing more, when suddenly I was jerked wide awake by realising that I was no longer on level boggy turf. I was slipping downhill on a stony slope, and below me was the sound of running water. I stood still thinking. I was probably near the stream that flowed to the lake, and if I could feel my way up to the source I might be able to find the path home—only I should have to be very careful not to fall into the lake. Anyhow, it seemed worth trying, so I took a few cautious steps and bumped into a tree. Yet I was sure it was my only hope of ever getting home, so I felt my way on, and the noise of the rushing water seemed to get nearer and nearer and louder all the time. I wondered how deep it was, and my fear came sweeping back over me; yet on I went, testing every step, till suddenly I stopped again, taken by surprise, for the ground was rising steeply, and the stones were slipping away behind me. I felt with my hands and began to guess where I was. I was almost sure that I was climbing a heap of loose shard, and I must be in the old quarry, near to the ruined house with the blackened walls and the empty staring windows.

My heart gave a leap of unreasonable terror, which passed quite quickly. For according to Johnny, someone lived in these ruins, and anyone at that moment was better than no one. Surely anyone on a night like this would take pity on a little lost girl and take her home. So I went on, scrambling upwards, conscious now of a new sound besides the rushing water. A soft warm wind was breathing up the valley, carrying that still, deadly mist before it. Perhaps I should soon be able to see where I was.

I seemed to have reached the top of the slag pile

and my eyes, peering through the darkness, could make out a solid mass ahead of me. Perhaps I was looking at it too intently and forgetting to feel with my feet, but the next moment I slipped and, because there was nothing but loose stones to hold on to, I went on slipping and slipping, gathering speed as I went. I think I must have fallen a long way, for I hardly remember stopping. The next thing I knew was that I was lying half in the water and half out of it, with my leg all twisted round the wrong way. The wind was blowing hard, the moon had pierced the mist, and in front of me rose the blackened walls.

I tried to move, but the pain made me feel sick. So once again in desperation I cupped my hands round my mouth and called, "Help, help! Oh, please help me!" and in my heart I echoed the cry to the One Who I knew was still close beside me. "Oh, Lord Jesus, now I can't go on any longer. Please send someone NOW!"

The echoes of my cry seemed borne on the wind far up the valley, and I lay holding my breath and listening. At first I could hear nothing but the wind and the water, but after a few minutes I heard the noise of slow, shuffling footsteps coming from inside the ruin.

"Help!" I shouted again. "Oh, please, help me!"

I saw the glow of a lantern framed in one of the window gaps and heard the creaking of the broken door. Someone was certainly coming, and, whoever it was, it was an answer to my desperate cry for help. I had not been forsaken. I had been led to this strange place, and now someone else was being led, slowly, stumbling over the slag toward me. I could hear the heavy boots kicking the stones and splashing through the water, and a voice I had heard before said, "Who's there?"

Why did that voice send such shivers down my spine? I caught my breath and seemed to lose the power to answer. The next moment he had raised the lantern above his head and was looking down into my face, and I was looking up into his—a haggard, sick, unshaven face—a face that I knew.

CHAPTER XX

THE RESCUE

WELL, I'LL BE BLOWED!" said the man, as we stared mutely at each other by the eerie light of the lantern. "Seems as though I can't shake you off, doesn't it! And what is it that you are doing here?"

I could not speak at first, my terror was too great. Was this the answer to my prayer? Had I been left to the mercy of this dreadful thief? I could only gaze up at him at first, my body rigid with fear, as still as a rabbit gazing at a snake. Perhaps he understood what I felt, for he spoke again quite gently, and the wild look in his eyes seemed to fade out.

"Now, now!" he said. "There's no call to look like that. I'm not going to hurt you. You're hurt already, aren't you?"

"Yes," I whispered between dry lips. "I think . . . I think I've broken my leg."

"Is that so?" he said, kneeling down beside me

and scanning me again with the lantern. "Well, I'm going to carry you into my house, and then you can tell me what brings you here."

I screamed with pain as he lifted me out of the stream bed, and clung to him desperately. He smelt of beer, and the weight of me seemed to exhaust him, for he breathed heavily as he plodded back to the ruin. He had left his lantern outside, but I felt myself being lowered very gently on to a mattress, and it was not pitch dark, for some ashes still glowed red in the stone fireplace in the middle of the room.

He left me and returned in a moment with the lantern. He was still very out of breath, and his face looked white and weary. He sat for a moment at the bottom of the mattress where I lay, holding his head in his hands. Then he turned round and stared at me again.

"Well," he said at last, "what do you think you are doing, spying on me like that?"

"I wasn't spying," I whispered pleadingly. "I . . . I didn't know you lived here. I got lost in the mist, and I fell over the quarry."

"You were following me," said the man, "you and that boy up on the moor. I saw you before you saw me. The boy followed me right up to the public house."

I was silent, for I had nothing to say. I just lay wondering if he would kill me.

A spasm of anger seemed to pass through him. "I could do away with you here, now, if I liked," he said, suddenly shaking his fist at me. Then, seeing my terror, his anger seemed to pass as swiftly as it had come. "But you need not be frightened. I am not going to hurt you at all, I am not. I had a little girl myself once. She turned out bad, and God only knows where she is now, but she was an innocent little bit of a thing like you once. Now I suppose if you're lost, every policeman in the district is out on the mountains looking for you . . . got me into a pretty fix, haven't you?" He sat staring into space, as though trying to make up his mind what do do.

"If you could go and fetch Mr. Owen from Davies's Farm," I faltered at last, "he'd take me home. I promise I'd never, never tell . . . no one would know I knew you."

"Oh, the boy's seen to that," said the man flatly. "I watched 'em go up to the Police Station together, him and that parson chap, but I thought I'd be safe here one more night. It was kind of dark for a getaway just then. Besides, I've nowhere to get away to . . . I'm finished . . . down and out. I'll be better off in prison when the bad weather comes, so here goes."

He rose to his feet, but still seemed uncertain what to do.

"That parson chap won't be at the farm now," he remarked, "he'll be out on the mountain looking for you. I'm going to get those wet clothes off you and wrap you in my blanket, and then I'll go up to the lake and call round a bit. The rain's coming up on the wind, and the sooner I go, the better."

He helped me out of my wet clothes as gently as a woman, and wrapped me in a thick warm blanket, which later turned out to be one of Mrs. Thomas's best Witney woollens. But I noticed none of these things at the time, for the pain in my leg was the only thing I could really think of.

"So long!" said the man, when he'd made me as comfortable as possible. "And put in a word for me when I'm taken. Remember I did my best for you."

I did not understand what he meant, but I murmured my thanks and lay in the dark staring at the tiny glowing patch of ashes. I was not afraid of this man any longer, for if he was a thief, he was a kind thief, and I did not want him to go to prison. But

I realised that by saving me he was giving himself up, and I felt terribly sorry about it.

I must have lain for a long time half dozing, conscious only of the pain and the beating of the rain all round me, for a storm had blown up. Fortunately the corner in which I lay was roofed over and dry, but the wind howled through the spaces in the wall, and to my fevered imagination the rushing water in the stream sounded as though it would carry me away. I was now shivering, now burning, and not very sure where I was. Sometimes I thought I was still on the moor, struggling through the mist, sometimes I thought I was away back in London, and heard my own voice crying out for Mrs. Moody to bring me a glass of water. I was parched with thirst and lost in a great blackness.

"Thou wilt show me the path . . . in Thy Presence . . . " Who was saying those words? No one, it was just the end of my nightmare. I had somehow forgotten the Presence, but He was still there, and I was suddenly fully conscious again that not for one minute had I been alone. The rain was still beating down, and the night was pitch black, but the love of God was all around me like light. "Fulness of joy," I whispered to myself, "I'm not a bit afraid any more . . . and I believe someone's coming."

I strained my ears to listen. Above the rain and the rushing water I could hear men's voices, and the next moment I saw the steady glow of a storm lantern through a window gap. The creaking of the old door, the sound of boots stumbling across the uneven floor, and the next moment the room was aglow with lantern light, and there was Mr. Owen looking almost as ill and haggard as the man who followed him.

"Elaine, my poor little girl!" he cried, kneeling down beside me. "Thank God I've found you! Are you hurt, dear? Can you tell me?"

I nodded. "My leg," I murmured, "and I'm thirsty. Please can I have a drink of water?"

He had already pulled a knapsack off his back containing warm clothes and food and a thermos of tea. I could not eat anything, but the tea was delicious, and so was the feel of dry clothing. I felt for his hand and closed my eyes. Now that he was there, I wanted nothing in the world but to go to sleep. The storm was still raging outside, and there was nothing to be done but to stay there till morning.

Although I slept fitfully, the pain kept waking me, and I lay drowsily watching Mr. Owen and the man. They had blown up the dying ashes to a warm blaze and were sitting in front of it.

"You'll always be a hunted man, even if you do get away," I heard Mr. Owen say. "Far better get it over; they are after you now, and if they catch you running away, they'll be hard on you. If you give yourself up, they'll be lenient. And I'll stand by you, and tell them what you did for our little girl." The man mumbled something in hopeless, broken tones, but I couldn't make out the words.

"But I'll be there waiting at the end of it," said Mr. Owen earnestly. "It won't be as it was before, no chance of starting again and not a friend in the world. I'll have a job waiting for you, and a home for you to come to. My wife and I will never forget what you've done to-night. Get it over, man, and start again. You are starving, aren't you? Have a sandwich."

I drifted back into an uneasy sleep, and when I woke again a pale light was stealing into the wretched room. The rain had stopped, and the sky over the slag heaps was faintly golden. The man lay fast asleep on the floor in front of the fire, and Mr. Owen sat with his head on his knees keeping watch over us both.

Hearing me stir, he rose stiffly to his feet and came over to me. He looked worn out with sleeplessness and anxiety; he had more hot tea ready and fed me like a baby, for my head was so hot and heavy that I could hardly raise it from the mattress. Then he drew back the blankets and examined my leg very gently.

"We shall have to get hold of a stretcher and an ambulance, Elaine," he said. "I think it is broken."

The light was so bright now that it hurt my head, and I shut my eyes. I cannot remember clearly what happened after that, but after a time I realised that Mrs. Owen was sitting beside me, and Mr. Owen had gone . . . and then there seemed to be a great many people in the ruin, and I felt a sharp stab of pain as I was lifted on to the stretcher, and after that I knew I was being carried downhill, for it bumped and jolted, and I felt the sunshine on my face and smelt the wet bracken and leaf mould all round me . . . and then we were all going somewhere in a car, but I was too tired to ask where, and although sometimes I heard my voice speaking, it seemed like someone else's saying words that were not mine. I was conscious of being carried indoors and seeing nurses gathering round me, and I kept putting out my hand to make sure Mrs. Owen was still there, but she always was, and I wondered what they were doing without her. And then I felt a prick in my arm and knew nothing more for a very long time.

I was very, very ill, so I learned later. Not only was my leg broken, but the long hours spent in running in wet clothes, the cold, the fall, and the fright had been too much for me, and for nearly a week I hung between life and death. Sometimes I was conscious of sharp pains in my chest, and I seemed to be fighting for breath, but most of the time I was dreaming and did not know where I was. Sometimes I was lost in thick white mists among dark rocks; sometimes I was falling, falling into bottomless blackness and then I would cry out. And always at my cry there were hands stretched out to hold me, and kind, strong, tender faces bent down over mine. Sometimes it was Mr. Owen, and sometimes Mrs. Owen, and sometimes above the rushing sound of water and the empty blackness I heard them saying words that seemed like lamps leading me home.

"The Lord is my Shepherd, I shall not want . . . Yea, though I walk through the valley of the shadow of death, I will fear no evil: for Thou art with me."

And once I woke from a lost, frightening dream and saw Janet's face, pale and tear-stained, looking down at me; the sky behind her, framed in the big ward windows, was bright with sunset. I learned afterwards that on that night they had wondered whether I would live, and Janet had begged so hard to see me that Mr. Owen had brought her over and left her to watch beside me for a few minutes.

"Janet," I asked, suddenly clear and sensible, "why are you crying? Am I going to die?"

She took my heavy little hand and pressed it against her wet cheek. Poor Janet! She never knew how to pretend or to say anything that wasn't the exact truth, so she answered my question quite simply.

"I don't know, Elaine. They say you might. But you needn't be frightened, you'd go straight to Jesus."

Her eyes overflowed again, and I felt her hot tears running down my hand. I stared beyond her at the open heavens flecked with crimson and gold. It seemed as though God had opened His gates wide, and the glory was stealing through.

"Of course not," I answered, struggling for breath to explain, "Fulness of joy" . . . then the mists closed round me again, and I fell asleep.

Then suddenly all the faces disappeared, and there was just one that was there all the time—my mother's face. But at first I hardly knew it, for it was no longer pretty and carefully made-up; it was pale and frantic with great dark circles under the eyes. And when I cried out in my dreams, she would clutch hold of me, and I felt her fear almost as strong as mine. Somehow we both seemed lost in the mist together, and I longed for the words that had been like lamps leading me home. So night followed day, and day followed night, and I dreamed, and cried, and woke, and dreamed again.

And then suddenly I woke up properly and knew I was not dreaming any longer. It must have been very early morning, for the windows were grey and the night nurse's shaded lamp was still burning in the middle of the ward. I raised myself on my elbow, and she came over to my bed at once.

"Where's my Auntie?" I asked her. Surely they hadn't all gone off and left me!

"Your mother's here, dear, sleeping in the side ward," said Nurse kindly. "I'll fetch her at once."

Mummy was at my side in a few moments, clad in a dressing-gown. She looked old and tired, and dreadfully frightened, and I had a strange feeling that it was Mummy who was lost in the mist, and I who must stretch out my hand and lead her home.

"Hallo, Mummy," I said calmly, "I'm better. Did you come because I was ill?"

"Oh, my darling," cried my mother, putting her arms round me and bursting into tears, "are you really better? I thought I was going to lose you, and I was so dreadfully frightened!"

I lay thinking. Apart from my leg, which was in plaster, I felt wonderfully cool and light. All the real things were very, very real, and nothing else mattered. I was still too ill to feel shy of anyone.

"I wasn't afraid," I answered. "I'd have gone to Jesus and fulness of joy. But now I'm going to get better instead. Please give me a drink, Mummy, I'm dreadfully thirsty."

The nurse had arrived with a tray of tea and biscuits for my mother, and she took my temperature and seemed delighted. She was pretty and curly, and I liked her. My mother fed me with a feeding cup, and I found I was hungry and ate two biscuits. Then, tired out, but still light and cool and at peace, I lay holding her hand, and the sweet Summer dawn came creeping in through the windows. The night nurse turned out the lamp, and the birds began to sing in the hospital garden.

CHAPTER XXI

THE PATH THAT LED HOME

ONCE I HAD TURNED THE CORNER, I got well rapidly, and my mother soon felt that she should be getting back to work. I was still in bed on the morning she left, and for the first time I brought up the subject of the Christmas holidays.

"We shall be leaving France in November, darling," she said, "and of course I'll come up for the week-end as soon as we reach England. And then it will only be another few months, and you'll be home for good. I'm already finding out about flats, and I'll get a fortnight's holiday over Christmas. What fun it will be to be together again!"

I lay very still. I did not want to hurt Mummy's feelings, but somehow she must understand. I wanted to see her on visits, but my home was here in the country now with Janet and Philippa, and I could not go back and live in London. But I did not know how to explain and, being very weak after my illness, the tears welled up in my eyes and I felt my lips trembling.

My mother stared at me, and went rather red. There was a long, uncomfortable silence.

"Do you not want to come home?" she asked in a light, hard voice. "Would you rather stay on and have Christmas with the Owens? They seem extremely fond of you, and it's just as you like, you know."

It was the chance I had been waiting for, but somehow I could not take it—I wasn't sure if Mummy was angry or just sad, but in any case I was too nervous to explain anything. I lay there looking miserable and twisting the sheet in my hands.

"Well," said my mother, "you've only to say so, it's exactly as you like."

"I . . . I don't know. I'll ask Auntie," I whispered. "I'll tell you later, Mummy."

"Oh, very well," answered my mother coldly, "but make up your mind soon, as I must make my plans as well as you." She glanced at her watch and yawned. "I must be going soon. Well, good-bye, darling, get better quickly. I'll be back in a few weeks."

She kissed me lightly and turned away. But the nurse stopped her at the ward door, and I caught a glimpse of her face and noticed tears on her cheeks. And I buried myself under the bed-clothes and cried and cried, but had anyone asked me why, I could not have said.

"I'll ask Auntie to explain," I thought to myself. "She'll be able to make Mummy understand." And with this I comforted myself and grew stronger every day, until one morning the doctor stopped quite casually at the bottom of my bed and said he thought I could go home, and the nurse told Auntie she could fetch me the next day after dinner.

Never shall I forget the day I went home.

I was allowed up after breakfast, and packed all my little affairs, and went hobbling round on my plaster saying goodbye to all the patients in turn, for being the only little girl in the ward I had become quite a favourite. Then I settled myself in an armchair, too excited to eat my dinner, and sat with my eyes glued to the clock till half-past two. After that I sat with my eyes glued to the door, and the eternity of waiting came to an end at last, for I suddenly saw Janet's rosy, smiling face peeping in, and behind her came Mrs. Owen and Peter, all looking almost as excited as I was.

The nurse, rather less starchy than usual, came out to the car and waved me off, and then at last

we were rolling out through the gates and away
into the world that I had not seen for nearly a
month, for my only view from the hospital had
been tidy lawns and brick chimneys. We motored
home the back way through country lanes and, although I did not know that the golden tang in the
air was the first breath of Autumn, I did notice
that the bracken on the hills was turning yellow,
and the mountain-ash trees were laden with berries, and the dahlias were blazing in the cottage
gardens. In fact, it seemed like a new world, and I
a new child, born afresh into its beauty and
liberty.

Mr. Owen, Blodwen, Johnny, Frances, Robin,
Lucy and Cadwaller were all at the gate under
an amazing white banner with the words "Welcome Home" stitched across it in uneven red flan-
nel letters, and the noise of their greeting must
have shaken the parish. But somehow we all got
in at the gate, and I was dragged down the path
by many loving little hands and in at the front
door, where another surprise awaited me. The
table was laid for a party, and the room was a mass
of late crimson roses, while on the couch by the
window lay Philippa, with her mother sitting beside her. The taxi that had fetched me had called

for her first, for she was determined to be there on the great day.

It was a wonderful party, better than Christmas, so Johnny remarked. We had ham sandwiches, chocolate biscuits, fruit salad, and a big cake, baked by Blodwen, iced by Janet, and with "Welcome Home, Elaine" printed on it in silver balls by Frances. And we talked and talked, because there was so much to say, and although we had all heard each other's adventures in couples, we now wanted to hear them individually. Peter had been most severely blamed for his share in my accident and was a little unwilling to talk about his doings. But in the end he was persuaded to tell how, supposing I'd simply turned back home, he had crept on across the moor, always keeping his quarry within hearing distance. He had tracked him right down to the little weaving village on the main road, where the man had tried to shake him off by going into the public house. But Peter, hovering about outside, had been picked up by Mr. Owen and Frances on their way home, and they had dropped into the local Police Station and reported the whole story to the chief constable, who promised to look into the matter. He knew the man slightly—a down-and-out tinker who tried to make a living by calling and soldering pots and pans at the outlying mountain farms. They had had their eye on him lately, but up to that time no one had proved anything against him.

Then Mr. Owen talked about the man who had been watching out of the pub. window, and who might have escaped, had he not stayed to go out on the hills and look for Mr. Owen. He had found him calling and searching at the entrance of the valley, while Mr. Davies, the shepherd, had already gone down for the police. All night long, while I slept my uneasy sleep, the two men had sat on the floor by that flickering little fire and talked things over. The man had poured out all his pitiful story: he had been an unwanted child, brought up by a drunken father, and had quickly got into bad ways. He had married, but his wife had left him, taking with her the only person he had really loved, his little girl. He had already been to prison once and had come out ill, without work, and without a friend in the world. Life had been a bitter, hopeless struggle ever since, and he was sick of it all and ready to give himself up. He made no secret about the robbery. The silver he had sold, but the blankets were still there, wrapped round me.

So he and Mr. Owen had gone to the Court together, and the previous week he'd been sen-

tenced to three months' imprisonment. But he had
gone quietly enough, knowing that at last he had
a friend who would stand by him all the way
through and be there waiting for him on the day
when the prison gates would open for him. For
Mr. Owen had promised to write to him every
week and visit him once a month, and already
he was looking out for a kind employer and a decent job.

We sat silent for a minute, thinking of the unwanted child battling alone, the friendless, hungry man tramping the mountains, the lonely pris-
oner in his cell, and perhaps each one lifted a
thought of gratitude to God for all the love and
safety and shelter He had poured so freely into
our lives. I glanced round at the happy, healthy
children, the good food we were eating, the
warm clothing we were wearing, the yellow evening sunshine streaming in at the window, and
wondered for an instant why we'd been given so
much. But just then Blodwen, glancing at the
clock, asked was she to cook any supper or was
she not, and we decided that we might just as well
go on with tea; and then it was my turn to tell
about my adventures, and they were the most exciting of all.

I think we could have talked all night, but

Mrs. Owen suddenly jumped up and said I'd been up too long for the first day and must go back to bed at once. So they all came to the bottom of the stairs to watch me climb up in my plaster leg, and the last I saw of them was a sea of rosy, laughing faces clustered in the hall, waving goodnight to me. And only when I reached my bedroom did I realise how tired I was, and how glad to tumble into bed.

Mrs. Owen helped me in and then went off to fetch me a last hot drink. It was wonderful to be back in my own little room and to know that I would wake up in the morning and see the yellowing beech trees through the open windows, and find Janet sleeping beside me. And then once again there rose up that unquiet thought in my heart, "Supposing I had to leave it; supposing I had to go back to London." Well, I wouldn't leave it; it was my home now, and Mummy had said I could do as I liked. Now was my chance to get things straight.

Mrs. Owen sat down on my bed while I drank my Ovaltine, and I plunged into the subject at once.

"Auntie," I said abruptly, "I never want to go back to London. I want to stay here now and have Christmas with you and go on going to school with Janet. Can you tell Mummy, 'cos she said I could do what I liked, and she would always come up and visit me?"

Mrs. Owen looked very troubled, and this surprised me, for it had all seemed perfectly simple to me.

"I couldn't tell her," she said. "If you really want to stay, you must talk it over between yourselves. Of course, we all want you to stay very badly, and we shall miss you dreadfully, but, you see, you are all your mother has got. Have you ever thought how lonely she would be without you?"

I was silent. I had not thought very much about her side of it. My own side mattered to me so much.

"I don't think we need decide to-night," she said quietly, "we must think about it. But don't forget your special verse. The Lord Jesus has got the path all planned out for you. Ask Him to show you very, very clearly where it is going to lead you, because only walking in that path will you find fulness of joy."

She kissed me and left me, and I buried my head in the pillows and said my prayers. But I did not ask to be shown the Path of Life. I just said,

"Please, please, let me stay here, because I could never be happy in London."

The Autumn weather was mellow and golden, and I grew strong again surprisingly quickly. By the beginning of October my plaster was off, and I was able to go back to school. The beeches turned brown and gold on the hillside, and we scuffled along in the russet fall and buried each other in the drifts. The blackberries had ripened on the crimson brambles, and we spent Saturday afternoon robbing the hedges. Blodwen made pounds of bramble jelly, and Peter was busy with a collection of fruits and berries for his museum.

I was able to climb the hill again and visit Philippa, and I looked forward to these visits, for a real change had come over her. One night, while the rest of us were at Camp, she had come to the Lord Jesus and asked Him to forgive her and make her His own little girl and to come into her heart, and since that day He had quite simply been teaching her that true happiness lies in making other people happy and in giving instead of getting. And day by day she was putting up a brave, steady fight against grumbling and selfishness, and winning victories over her crossness and self-pity. She worked hard at her lessons now, and had learned to knit, and was always thinking of things she could do for other people. Mr. Owen used to visit her and tell her about the parish, and she had started to knit bootees for the new babies and to print little letters and verses for people who were ill or in trouble. Her mother rejoiced at the change in her and to my surprise seemed to think it was something to do with me.

It was on a cool, clear day towards the end of October that I was sitting on the window-sill talking to Philippa. The flower beds were a mass of Michaelmas daisies and chrysanthemums, and the little cherry tree against the wall flamed like a lamp. Philippa and I had been making a toadstool garden with a tin lid full of moss, and evening was drawing in. It was nearly time to go home.

"Elaine," said Philippa suddenly, "when have you got to go back to your mother in London?"

The old fear leaped up in my heart, for November was drawing on, and Mummy would soon be coming. But I felt sure it would be all right. After all, she had said I could do as I liked.

"I'm not going back," I answered. "Mummy said I could choose. I'm going to stay here. I could never be happy in London."

Philippa's clear blue eyes, that sometimes seemed to see so much more than I wanted them to see, were looking straight at me in contemptuous surprise.

"Well, I'm bothered!" she exclaimed. "You told me that if I belonged to the Lord Jesus, I could be happy with lame legs, and I went and believed you. And now you say that you couldn't even be happy in London. Legs is far, far worse than London!"

Her words seemed to hit me, and I had no answer to give at all, but I tried to think out some excuse.

"Oh, but if I went back to London, there'd be no one to teach me about Jesus," I stammered. "My mother doesn't know much about the Bible."

"Well, neither does mine," said Philippa firmly. "But she's awfully pleased I've stopped being so cross, and I told her it was knowing about Jesus. So now she thinks the Bible must be a very good book, and she comes and reads it with me. But all the same, Elaine, I really do hope you don't go away, because I shall miss you so dreadfully."

"Well, it isn't quite decided," I said slowly, rising to my feet. New thoughts were flocking into my mind, and I felt I must get way and think things over. I said a hasty goodbye, but I didn't go home. I climbed the lamb pasture and sat down on the roots of a mighty beech tree, and cupping

my face in my hands I gazed out over the land,
sniffing in all the vivid scents of a clear October
evening: dying leaf mould, freshly turned earth
and the haunting smell of wood smoke rising in
blue spirals from the bonfires at the farms.

I could see a long way. Just below me were the
golden woods, and beyond them the brown
ploughed fields. Mr. Jones was still clanking to and
fro behind his horses, turning the last furrow,
and the gulls wheeled behind him, the last sun
rays kissing their wings; and beyond that was the
opal line of the sea and the pale evening sky. This
was my home, the broad fruitful land I'd learned
to love. How could I leave it?

I turned and looked behind me. The far hills
seemed very near to-night, and on one of them I
could see a lonely little path winding up over the
rocks and twisting through the yellow bracken.
It seemed to run right to the top of the crest and
to meet the sunset. All I had ever learned about my
verse flashed into my mind at that moment. "Thou
wilt show me the Path of Life . . . "—the path that
Jesus had planned for me—"In Thy Presence"—
travelling hand in hand with the Lord Jesus along
that path "is fulness of joy," and I seemed to hear
Philippa's scornful voice—"You say you couldn't
ever be happy in London."

"Lord Jesus," I whispered, "show me the Path. I really want to know."

And, as I sat waiting for my answer, I began to think about my mother—my pretty, clever, capable mother, who went to France and gave parties and rushed off in aeroplanes and always seemed to know what to do and how to do it. And yet in hospital she had been desperately afraid, and I remembered her frightened face and the funny feeling I'd had that Mummy was lost in the mist, and I must put out my hand and lead her home. And there was no one else. The Owens all had one another, but Mummy had only me.

I looked back at the path. The sunset had faded, and I could no longer see where it led, but the peace of the blue dusk brooded over it, and very soon the stars would come out. A lonely little path winding up to the skyline, and beyond the skyline were the great mountains.

I turned and went downhill, still limping a little. Across the shadowed fields I saw two figures coming towards me. Mrs. Owen had started out to look for me, and fat Lucy was toddling beside her. We met by the first beech tree, and I slipped my hand into hers.

"There's a letter from your mother," said Mrs.

Owen a little hesitatingly. "She's coming up to see you on Saturday to talk things over."

I looked up with the light of certainty on my face.

"Good," I said, "I'm glad she's coming. I'm going back to London at the end of term to live with her."

There was a moment's silence. Perhaps Mrs. Owen was waiting for me to explain, but I'd said all I had to say.

"Did you find out? . . . Is it the Path of Life?" she asked softly at last.

I nodded.

"Then you'll find fulness of joy," she said, stooping to pick up Lucy. And hand in hand we strolled home through the dark fields, and the lights shone out in a cosy glow from the Vicarage windows ahead of us.

Moody Press, a ministry of the Moody Bible Institute, is designed for education, evangelization and edification. If we may assist you in knowing more about Christ and the Christian life, please write us without obligation to: Moody Press, c/o MLM, Chicago, Illinois 60610.